Online Dispute Resolution

An International Business Approach to Solving Consumer Complaints

Foreword by
Jo DeMars

Edited by
Colin Adamson

Project Coordinated by
Net Neutrals EU

authorHOUSE®

AuthorHouse™
1663 Liberty Drive
Bloomington, IN 47403
www.authorhouse.com
Phone: 1 (800) 839-8640

Published by AuthorHouse 11/25/2015

ISBN: 978-1-5049-6355-8 (sc)
ISBN: 978-1-5049-6354-1 (e)

Library of Congress Control Number: 2015919346

Print information available on the last page.

Table of Contents

Foreword

Complaint handling has always been a business for pragmatists. Labouring largely unrecognised in the back offices or outsourced call centres of their employers, these foot soldiers of what was hailed as the great revolution of 'putting the customer first' have had little to guide them in their endeavours in the way of theory or specific statute. Theirs was a practical business focused on trying to satisfy the customer or if that failed, shutting them up or ignoring them in the hope they would eventually go away even if it was to a rival concern.

There was however one source of enlightenment – US data from way back in the 70's that suggested that complaint handling could contribute to profit and growth. That sparked a wave of investment and interest in the function of complaint management that lasts to this day. TARP the consultancy who collected and promoted these findings exported this message abroad – setting up their European arm in the '80s.

This book celebrates that continuing interest and its application across many markets. It is written at a moment of anticipation when alternative dispute resolution and its technological handmaiden are being actively encouraged in the countries of the European Union. Effective resolution of consumer complaints in ways which are accessible, low cost, fair and technically agile is attracting unprecedented support from governments and businesses at both national and international levels.

This book is as I said a celebration and one which has drawn together a diverse and talented set of authors – veterans and not so veterans of complaint handling from different perspectives and also newer activists contemplating new ways of working – using the law if that works but very ready to contemplate other ways of working if that works better.

So we are back to pragmatism again. A definition of complaint handling which has always rung true for me is "bargaining in the shadow of the law". Now we are looking at new ways of doing that and doing it across national boundaries – not just the free movement of goods and services, but the free movement of legal decisions that make it easy for people using new technology to buy things, to use that technology to help them when things go wrong.

The book is ordered to illuminate different aspects of the developments I have outlined above. Marc Grainer was with his colleague John Goodman (and later Colin Adamson in Europe) the first to propound the thesis that complaint handling pays. It seems right therefore that his chapter heads up our book asking whether the bright new dawn for investment in better complaint handling has in fact yielded the benefits we hoped would follow. If it has not, what can business do about it? His ideas are an ideal starting point.

My chapter that follows intentionally narrows the focus to the here and now on the newer methodologies for satisfying disappointed customers that take account of the changes in the way that people shop and act if things go wrong. There are many different approaches and I have tried to round them up for the reader – especially the non-US ones who may be unfamiliar with the experience we have had in the definition and application of ODR (online dispute resolution).

The EU is launching innovative schemes with its Digital Strategy designed to create the confidence amongst its millions of consumers that is necessary before they embark on cross-border shopping to take advantage of the spread and diversity not just of prices but of the goods and services themselves available in the 28 countries in that single market. Pablo Cortez of Leicester University in the UK has made online dispute resolution his speciality and he with two other academic colleagues from the Universities of Barcelona and Helsinki respectively set out the legal frameworks being built as well as the obstacles the proposed arrangements have to address in areas such as enforcement and the design of the technologies to support ADR/ODR.

To show what can be achieved by adapting technology, we have an example of a programme which has helped many people facing one of the most grave problems for consumers and their families – the repossession of their home. We are not talking here of a faulty food-mixer. In her account of a mediation programme set up in the aftermath of the mortgage crisis in 2007, Amy Koltz takes us through the process involved in working with multiple stakeholders to achieve the goals of this important programme. Technology contributes a lot but you have to get the human beings on board first.

The hopes and dreams of how things will work in the future must pay heed to the realities of what is happening now and it seemed the moment to go back to the nitty gritty – what Katherine Newcomer and other complaint managers like her have to contend with and decide upon on a daily basis. Not for nothing did we call her chapter 'Abuse, Truth, Fraud and Fairness' – all human life is there. Considering the parade of human vanity and emotion that cross her screen every day I thought her treatment was very restrained.

Finally we end on a note of anticipation and speculation with Adrian Lawes wandering lonely as a cloud (for those of you who like Wordsworth) across the landscape of the UK speculating about the public's reaction to the new approaches on offer.

I hope you learn from this collection of talents and topics. I look forward to working with you.

- Jo DeMars

A Promise Unfulfilled and What to Do About It – Complaint Handling Now

Marc Grainer; Scott Broetzmann, David
Beinhacker, and Richard Grainer

*Marc Grainer currently serves as Chairman of Customer
Care Measurement and Consulting*

Research (the White House Study) commissioned by the U.S. Office of Consumer Affairs conducted in 1976 found that there was an uplift in brand loyalty (compared to that of non-complainants) when customers complained about their problems with products and services (see note 1). This was the case even when complaints were not satisfactorily resolved. As a result of these findings, companies have spent billions of dollars on upgraded complaint-handling practices over the past 39 years. Has this considerable promise of complaint-handling, as an effective retention marketing strategy, paid off for business and its customers?

Unfortunately, research such as the Customer Rage Studies carried out by Customer Care Measurement and Consulting, LLC (CCMC) and the W.P. Carey School of Business, Arizona State University (ASU), during 2003 – 2013, has documented the aggregate poor performance of business to satisfy complaints (see note 2). This study found that complainant satisfaction is lower today than it was in 1976 (41% vs. 44%). To make matters worse, now when complaints are not satisfactorily resolved, brand loyalty decreases. Today it only pays to handle complaints if business satisfies the complaining consumers.

Therefore, much of the early promise of corporate complaint-handling as a positive marketing strategy remains unfulfilled.

A Road Map for Increasing Complainant Satisfaction

Nonetheless, there is some cause for optimism. A road map does exist for improving complainant satisfaction, and these recommendations will cost business little, and in some cases will actually save money. If these recommendations are adopted by business, it is not unreasonable to project an aggregate national increase of 10 to 15 percentage points of complainant satisfaction. This road map of best practices consists of six sets of recommendations.

<u>1. Proper Use of the Telephone</u>

CCMC's 2013, the Customer Rage Study reported 67% of complainants using the telephone as their primary channel for complaining. Therefore, a key to improving satisfaction rests with the proper use of the telephone to handle complaints.

The 2005/2006 research labelled The Conventional Wisdom Study catalogued the telephone complaint-handling practices that customers liked and disliked (see note 3). Using a 0-10 point scale (where "10" meant "WOULD SIGNIFICANTLY INCREASE YOUR SATISFACTION'" and "0" meant "WOULD SIGNIFICANTLY DECREASE YOUR SATISFACTION"), a sample of customers, who had submitted telephone complaints about product/service problems during the preceding year, rated the influence of 85 complaint-handling practices on their satisfaction. The objective of this study was to determine the validity of those assumptions that are the basis for contemporary complaint-handling practice.

The Negative

Scores from this study that were 2.50 and below are considered to be strongly negative. Five sets of complaint-handling practices that fall into this negative territory bear special mention.

First, many call centres that handle complaints try to piggyback sales campaigns onto their response to customer problems. The thought is that, once the company has the customer on the telephone, it's possible to "kill two birds with one stone."

While from a productivity standpoint such practices may seem to make sense, the findings from the Conventional Wisdom Study argue strongly against mixing sales efforts with complaint-handling. Selling after resolving the problem (1.58), selling before resolving the problem (1.23), and continuing to sell after being told "no" (1.01) were among those complaint-handling practices that caused the most dissatisfaction.

Second, telephone technology was another area that caused dissatisfaction. Examples of such practices were "when they transfer you to another department, you have to use an automated telephone system before you talk with an agent" (2.43), "you're told how to reach a person only after you've had to listen to a long message" (2.15), and "when you must use an automated telephone system, there's no option to talk to a person" (1.19). Complainant satisfaction suffers when companies make it difficult to talk to live agents.

Third, agent response practices like talking too fast and an inability to understand agents because of their accents received strongly negative ratings of 2.38 and 1.98, respectively.

The speed problem is often as a result of setting unrealistically high agent call-handling quotas. When this is the case, the data suggest that quality is more important than quantity. Handling fewer calls well is better than closing more calls badly. Productivity at the cost of complainant satisfaction will rarely translate into increased brand loyalty.

Accent is a more complex issue. In some cases, accent can impede understanding. Failure to successfully communicate with customers makes it difficult to resolve their complaints. Accent can also suggest outsourcing outside the United States; another significant cause of dissatisfaction that has been echoed in European findings where such outsourcing e.g. to India is also common.

While training can sometimes improve agent response practices (proper greetings, anger diffusion techniques, etc.), speed and accent problems are more often the result of strategic call centre policies; not a deficiency in agent skills. In this instance, misplaced productivity and cost concerns can result in lower complainant satisfaction.

Fourth, on the basis of anecdotal data, one of the most maddening customer care practices is having to repeat information that has already been provided. This ranges from customers having to repeat long numeric ID numbers to being asked to restate the reason why they're calling. In this instance, the anecdotal data mirrors Conventional Wisdom Study results. Having to repeat information received a strongly negative score of 2.15.

Basic case tracking software should preclude the need to repeat case-related information when the caller is transferred to a second agent or when the customer makes a follow-up call. Numeric ID's are often used to access information from the company's customer database. If these links are in place, customers should not have to be asked for their numeric ID twice. Most modern call centres, then, should not need to ask their customers to unnecessarily repeat information.

Fifth, as would be expected, remedy has the greatest impact on complainant satisfaction. Getting "none of the things you ask for" received the lowest score of the 85 complaint-handling practices that were being rated; a strong negative score of 0.66

In the real world, of course, resolution of customer complaints is not necessarily an all or nothing proposition. While it may not be feasible to give complainants everything they want, it is generally possible to give complaining customers something (partial monetary compensation, an apology, an opportunity to vent, etc.). Getting partial resolution to the customers' problems scored 3.55. Although, still a negative rating, this complaint-handling practice received a score more than five times higher than giving complainants nothing.

The Positive

Scores from the Conventional Wisdom Study of 7.50 and above are considered to be strongly positive. These customer preferences covered a wide range of complaint-handling practices.

The positive side of remedy ("you get everything you ask for") has the strongest influence on satisfying complainants. This received a score of 8.92; the highest rating given to any of the 85 telephone complaint-handling practices.

Agent response practices also strongly influence complaint satisfaction. Follow through on promises (8.91), agent knowledge (8.85), courtesy (8.72), empowerment (8.65), 24/7 agent availability (8.63), use of plain English (8.43), and agents telling complainants their names (7.87) all scored in the strongly positive range.

Ease of finding the number to call in order to reach the offending company is another strong positive influence on complainant satisfaction. Putting the number on the product, on the bill, product packaging, and product advertising all received scores above 7.50.

Other telephone practices that received strong positive scores included; being given a unique case reference number if there is a need to call back (8.15), timeliness of response (8.55), being told how long it will take to resolve the complaint (8.34), being able to contact the same agent if the complaint can't be resolved in one contact (7.76) and, when the call is initially answered by an automated response system, being given the option to talk to a live agent at the beginning of the instructions (7.87).

Recommendation

The Conventional Wisdom Study identified 16 strongly negative and 27 strongly positive telephone complaint-handling practices. Whenever possible, companies should avoid these negative practices and adopt the positive ones.

2. Say No to Ping-ponging; But Yes to First Contact Resolution

One of the key metrics used to assess corporate complaint-handling practices is the rate of first contact resolution. The White House Study found that 33% of complainants made only one contact to the place where the offending product/service was purchased. Thirty plus years later, the rate of first contact resolution as reported by the 2003 – 2013 Customer Rage Studies has dropped to 20%.

The importance of first contact resolution is recognized by the Conventional Wisdom Study. This complaint-handling practice was given the fourth highest rating of the 85 telephone practices being assessed with a score of 8.81.

All things being equal, the fewer contacts complainants need to make to resolve their problems; the higher the level of satisfaction. The 2003 – 2013 Customer Rage Studies reported substantial drops in complainant satisfaction when the customer found it necessary to make multiple contacts. There was a drop from 60% complainant satisfaction for one contact to 48% when two contacts were required. Only 34% of complainants were satisfied when three or more contacts were reported.

The irony for business is that the greater the number of contacts; the higher the administrative cost incurred and the more monetary remedy that is needed to resolve the complainant's problem. Therefore, many businesses are spending the bulk of their complaint handling budgets on those customers who are the least satisfied, who will be the least brand loyal in the future, and who are responsible for the most negative word of mouth.

A somewhat more sensitive metric is ping-ponging (the average number of contacts needed to resolve a complaint). This metric better takes into account any skew towards multiple contacts. Here again the average ping-ponging rate reported by the White House Study (3.5 contacts) is lower than that found thirty-plus years later by the Customer Rage Studies (4.1 contacts).

Recommendation

In order to improve complainant satisfaction, business should increase first contact resolution and decrease the rate of ping-ponging. First contact resolution targets should be above 50%. Ping-Pong rates should be below 1.5. (Of course, companies that handle complex complaints dealing with expensive products/services will generally score worse on these metrics than businesses handling simple problems with small ticket items.)

The trick to improving performance on such metrics is to assign realistic improvement targets and let management formulate product/company-specific policies designed to achieve these objectives. The key is tailoring the remedial policies to fit every company's unique needs.

3. The Power of Non-monetary Remedies

Data from the 2004 – 2013 Customer Rage Studies report an intriguing relationship between the type of remedy received and complainant satisfaction. Not surprisingly, those who felt they got only non-monetary remedies reported the lowest level of satisfaction (21%). Those who received only monetary remedies nearly doubled their level of complainant satisfaction to 37%. What is more interesting, though, is the satisfaction uplift reported by complainants who got both monetary and non-monetary remedies. Here the level of complainant satisfaction increased to 74%.

Providing both monetary and non-monetary remedies, then, recognizes that to resolve customer complaints, business must deal with both fixing the offending product/service problems as well as with addressing customer emotions. Best practice is to use apologies, opportunities to vent, etc. to defuse customer rage. Use of such techniques can significantly shorten the staff time required to handle especially difficult problems; thereby decreasing personnel costs.

Recommendation

Whenever feasible, business should offer complainants both monetary and non-monetary redress.

1. Review Outsourcing

Outsourcing the handling of customer complaints has been a growing trend over the last two decades. The logic for this policy is twofold.

First, companies outsource as a cost containment strategy. Outsourcing agencies argue that they offer savings on personnel, facilities, technology, etc.

Second, the trend in recent years has been for business to concentrate on core competencies. Most companies do not have a core competency in best practice complaint-handling. This is most often the case in areas such as customer care personnel and telephone technology. The argument, then, is that outsourcing agencies can offer higher quality complaint handling services.

While school is still out on the validity of these rationales, the Conventional Wisdom Study provides a complainant perspective on outsourcing. Here the reaction to outsourcing was decidedly negative. Outsourcing outside the United States received a strong negative rating for both telephone (2.01) and email (2.17) complaint handling. Even the general concept of outsourcing ("using an outside agency to answer your complaint") was viewed negatively (a 3.29 score for telephone and 3.08 for email complaints).

Evidence that business has begun to recognize the marketing disadvantages of outsourcing overseas is found in a television ad campaign by the U.S. mobile phone provider Consumer Cellular. These ads stress the fact that Consumer Cellular's products come "with great customer support, right here in the U.S." Plusnet a UK broadband supplier makes great play of locating its call centre not just in the United Kingdom but specifically in Yorkshire −the home of plain speaking. Further, most of the automobile companies that outsourced overseas have brought their call centres back to the U.S.

The savings from outsourcing overseas are largely based on the low personnel costs in these international complaint-handling centres. Such savings, however, can be illusory.

For example, international centres often have higher ping-pong rates. (More customer call backs are required to resolve the product/service problem than would be the case in a comparable U.S. centre.) Because companies are typically charged by the call, not the case, the true cost of resolving the customers' complaint may be camouflaged.

Done correctly, outsourcing should be transparent to the complainant. When transparent, these negative feelings toward outsourcing should not be a cause of complainant dissatisfaction.

Unfortunately, transparency is all too often absent. Accent, lack of product/service knowledge, incorrect grammar, lack of empowerment, etc. are examples of the factors that may suggest to complainants that their problems are being handled by outsourcing agencies.

When Ford first established its complaint-handling call centre, it used this centre as a training ground for new hires who would ultimately be assigned to other departments (e.g. the field organization) of the company. This year to two year assignment created a cadre of future executives that had been sensitized to customer needs. When Ford outsourced its call centre function, this OJT training vehicle was lost.

Recommendation

Before deciding to outsource the complaint handling function, business must weigh any of the potential benefits against complaints' negative attitudes toward this policy. If the decision is to outsource, this doesn't mean that a company should wash its hands of any complaint handling responsibility. On the contrary, management oversight of the outsourcing agency is extremely important. Formulating response rules, content of training programs, timely provision of remedies, and satisfaction surveys are among those areas where providing such oversight is critical.

2. Satisfaction Surveys: Do the Right Thing

Satisfaction surveys of complainants have become a standard tool for evaluating the performance of customer care agents, administrative support systems (e.g. telephone technology), and response rules. Used correctly, data gleaned from such surveys can serve as an important management tool.

The Conventional Wisdom Study addressed what impact fielding these surveys had on complainant satisfaction. The results from this study provided a mixed set of reviews.

For telephone complaints, asking the complainant "if you are satisfied with (the) response before ending the call" (rated 6.60) and "they ask you to take a satisfaction survey a few days or weeks after you've called for help" (5.70) had a positive influence on complainant satisfaction. Survey practices that had a more negative impact on satisfaction included: "you're invited to take a satisfaction survey at the end of the call, using an automated telephone system" (4.33), "they encourage you to say you're completely satisfied if you receive a satisfaction survey "(3.83), and "they don't address your concerns after you use a survey to tell them you're dissatisfied" (1.62)

Similar findings were reported for email complainants. While being requested to participate in a survey (5.06) had a neutral impact on complainant satisfaction, being coached (asking complainants to respond that they are completely satisfied) and not addressing problems raised in responses to a survey, had negative (3.80) and strongly negative (1.45) impacts, respectively, on satisfaction.

On occasion, satisfaction surveys may be designed in ways that measure complainant satisfaction incompletely. For example, surveys administered at the end of a complaint call are effective tools for assessing agent performance but don't measure the impact of remedies that are to be delivered in the future. (e.g., It may be days after the call is completed before it is possible to determine whether the defective product has been fixed.) Both process and outcome measures are necessary to accurately gage the level of complainant satisfaction.

In other instances, survey instrumentation may be a problem (e.g. use scales that are biased toward the positive). Such surveys can be designed to produce high scores and not accurately measure performance. This most often happens when complainant satisfaction is tied to financial incentives or is used in advertising campaigns.

Finally, some surveys try to measure too much. As a result of asking too many questions and not focusing on those relatively few items that are the key drivers of complainant satisfaction, management may direct remedial action towards improving performance in low scoring areas that have little influence on satisfaction.

Recommendation

When fielding satisfaction surveys, business should refrain from coaching complainants and respond to any problems raised by returned questionnaires. Further, basic rules of survey design should be followed in order to accurately measure complainant satisfaction.

3. Effective Use of the Internet as a Channel for Complaining

The Customer Rage Studies reported that the internet is still not a major channel for complaining. Only 4% of complainants designated the web as their primary channel for complaining in 2003. Internet usage for complaining had only increased to 7% by 2013. While the trend is upwards, the internet is still no match for the telephone as the primary channel most customers use for submitting complaints to business.

When the effectiveness of internet vs. telephone complaint handling practices was compared, in terms of complainant satisfaction, there was not a much of a difference. Forty-three percent of telephone vs. 41% of internet complainers were satisfied.

Next, the 2011 Customer Rage Study included two sets of questions that focused solely on internet usage.

First, complainants were asked whether they had posted information about their most serious problem on any of four specified types of websites (the offending company's site, social networking sites, social media sites, and/or sites that review products/services). Twenty-seven percent had posted on at least one of these sites. By 2013, this percentage had escalated to 45%. While not complaining behaviour per se, these postings often contain information about the complaining experience.

When asked why they posted on these sites, more than half of the reasons given related to deterring others from having similar bad experiences. This suggests that business should be concerned about the potential of market damage resulting from such postings.

Second, the study found that internet users can be quite discerning interpreters of the information they receive via the web. When social networking users were asked whether postings about good or bad experiences with products/services had the most influence on their future purchasing decisions, good experiences were designated as most influential by a margin of more than two to one (46% to 19%). Further, by a margin of 53% to 33% these respondents were more likely to post information about good as opposed to bad experiences.

Finally, recent developments in the field of ODR may offer some encouraging news regarding the potential of the web as a tool to facilitate the handling of customer complaints. Online companies have developed systems for promoting a more positive experience when customers complain. Modria, a US based software development company with a world-wide presence, offers a dispute management tool for corporations to employ internally. Modria has created a process that enables consumers to file a complaint electronically and receive a proposed solution automatically generated by the system. This product is based on a similar process developed for eBay which reportedly settles 60 million disputes each year. Capable of collecting data on the individual consumer, such as buying history or special needs, the system incorporates the personalized data to design individualized solutions. This personalized capability, along with the 24/7 availability of the system, may have the potential to positively impact customer relationship management.

Recommendation

While the use of the Internet for complaining is increasing, it would be a mistake for business to disproportionately invest in this channel. This is especially true given the fact that complaining via the web provides no advantage in complainant satisfaction. The investment decision will of course depend on the nature of the business and the product/service sold. An eBbay-style business will use the web much more often than a conventional bricks and mortar concern.

Nevertheless, forcing customers to use the web may be a short sighted policy. Business should be concerned that any cost savings resulting from channelling complainants to the web may be offset by the increased dissatisfaction of customers who find it easier to use other preferred channels to complain. Customers should be allowed to use the channels of their choice.

This has been the approach that has been taken by Esurance. Although this insurance company's business model stresses use of the internet, the theme of its advertising campaigns has been that the customer has a choice of channels, "People when you want them, technology when you don't." The tagline to its marketing campaign has been "insurance for the modern world, click or call."

While the web still may not be the primary channel for submitting complaints, the 2011 Customer Rage Study does find that postings about customer problems reach a wide audience. To date, much of business' concern has focused on deterring/removing negative postings. The 2011 survey, however, suggests that these efforts may be somewhat misplaced. Instead, the data suggest that a higher priority should be given to promoting the posting of positive experiences. Upgraded complaint handling practices can be an effective means for increasing such positive postings.

Further, companies should explore the feasibility of utilizing online dispute resolution tools as a means for both better personalizing and expediting responses to customer complaints.

So What: Why Should Business Care About Upgrading Its Customer Complaint Handling Practices?

There are two marketing-related reasons why business should care: 1) the retention of existing customers and 2) conquest sales to new customers. It is worth our while to remind ourselves of both the risks and rewards of this area of business performance by looking at the latest U.S. data.

Big Numbers

First, extrapolating from the 2013 Customer Rage Study data to the U.S. population as a whole, 56,000,000 households experienced at least one product/service-related problem during the twelve months preceding the survey (% of problem incidence x number of U.S. households). This translates into an eye-popping revenue at risk to business of $75,992,000,000 (number of households experiencing at least one product/service problem during the twelve months preceding the survey x the mean cost of those products/services that caused these households' most serious customer problems). Given today's low levels of complainant satisfaction, much of this revenue is not being recovered by business.

Revenue of Risk

The revenue at risk calculated here only applies to households' most serious problems. When households' less serious problems are considered, the total yearly revenue at risk would be substantially higher.

The Importance of Word of Mouth

Second, one of the most effective marketing tools available to business for winning new customers is word of mouth communications to friends, neighbours, relatives, etc. In the 2013 Customer Rage Study, households reporting problems told an average of 19.2 people about their experience. Again, given the low levels of complainant satisfaction, most of these communications were negative. (Sixty percent of the word of mouth reported by complainants in the 2007 – 2013 Customer Rage Studies was negative.) With the advent of posting on the internet, one person can now reach many thousands or more with a few key strokes.

In sum, those businesses that don't handle complaints effectively put their market share at significant risk. They stand to lose both existing and future customers.

Cost-Effective Remedies

This does not mean that business should give in to unreasonable customer demands. On the contrary, business should always do a cost-benefit analysis where the cost of the remedy is balanced against the value of the customer's future patronage/word of mouth communications. If there is nothing that can be done to save the unhappy customers' future patronage or to mitigate their negative word of mouth, the value of the remedy offered should be minimized. However, because the demands of most complainants are reasonable, a complaint based marketing strategy can be very successful.

Conclusion

The White House Study from the mid-1970's found a positive relationship between complaining and brand loyalty. On the basis of this finding, businesses substantially increased their investment in corporate complaint-handling practices.

The Customer Rage Studies (2003-2013) found that today the relationship between complaining and brand loyalty is not quite so clear cut. It now only pays to solicit complaints if the customer ends up being satisfied.

The good news, however, is that satisfying complainants still results in enough increased incremental brand loyalty to form the basis of a meaningful retention marketing strategy. The bad news is that the early promise of upgraded complaint-handling practices remains largely unfulfilled. The investment in expanded corporate programs has not paid off in increased complainant satisfaction. On the contrary, satisfaction has actually decreased over the past 30-plus years.

The primary reason satisfaction has not increased is that, all too often, companies "do all the right things, the wrong way." The programs being utilized by business to handle complaints are basically sound. The fault lies less with these programs but more with issues of poor execution.

Findings from the Customer Rage and Conventional Wisdom Studies do, however, provide some basis for optimism. A road map of six recommendations is proposed that, if adopted, could improve aggregate national complainant satisfaction by 10-15 percentage points. Implementing these recommendations would cost business little or nothing. In fact, some probably would save business money (e.g., decreased ping-ponging).

It should be possible to retain billions of dollars of future sales that business might otherwise have lost. This optimism is based on the premise that only by improving PERFORMANCE will the original promise of upgraded corporate complaint-handling practices ever be fulfilled.

Chapter Notes

1. For a detailed description of the findings from this survey, see A National Survey of Complaint-Handling Practices Used by Consumers, NTIS PB-263-82 (Washington, D.C.: U.S. Office of Consumer Affairs, 1976). This research was a national probability, in-home survey of 2,513 households.

2. The results of the first Customer Rage Study were released in 2003 in the Customer Care Alliance working paper, Grainer, Marc, Broetzmann, Scott, and Cormier, Cynthia; "Customer Complaint Handling – The Multibillion Dollar Sinkhole" and in Grainer, Marc, Broetzmann, Scott, and Cormier, Cynthia, "Checkmate: Complaint Handling at an Impasse with Rage," Customer Relationship Management, pp. 12 – 16, October, 2003, Volume VIII, Number 5. In recent years, CCMC has released the results of the Customer Rage Studies at ASU's Compete Through Service Symposiums (e.g., In 2013, "Will We Ever Learn?: The Sad State of Customer Care in America"). A detailed presentation comparing findings from 2013 with those from the previous five waves of the Customer Rage Studies can be found at www.customercaremc.com. The seventh wave of the Customer Rage Studies is being fielded during the summer of 2015.

3. This telephone survey of 701 respondents was fielded in late 2005 and early 2006. In addition to rating telephone complaint-handling practices, this study also rated 62 e-mail complaint-handling practices. These ratings can be found on CCMC's web site (www.customercaremc.com) in the 2011 working paper, Grainer, Marc, Broetzmann, Scott, and Beinhacker, David, "Why the Customer Care Revolution Failed: The Fallacy of Conventional Wisdom."

Online Dispute Resolution - Designing Systems for Effective Dispute Settlement – a US practitioner perspective

Jo DeMars

Owner & President of DeMars & Associates, a firm specialising in Alternative Dispute Resolution for more than 25 years

Case Study

In 2004 the Sellers on eBay Motors requested a dispute resolution process be developed to provide a review regarding the fairness of feedback left by Buyers. Some Sellers reported Buyers had figured out that they could use the threat of delivering negative feedback to persuade the Seller to give them a better deal.

For example, imagine a Buyer bids on a car, wins the auction, completes the transaction, then contacts the Seller a few days later and says, "I like the car, but I'd like it better if it had upgraded wheels. If you give me the cash for better wheels I'll leave positive feedback. If you don't, I'll probably have to say you refused to make me a happy customer."

Sellers are all too aware that negative feedback has the strong potential to turn away many would-be buyers. Not wanting to risk the costs of a bad reputation, which might take months to repair, the Seller may decide to grudgingly give in to the Buyer.

eBay looked into the situation and decided to offer an Independent Feedback Review (IFR) for feedback disputes. eBay concluded the credibility of the scheme would be increased if it was provided by a third party, in other words, it would be managed outside of the Company.

The IFR scheme has been in effect since October 2004. In 2013 it was expanded to cover US feedback disputes in all eBay categories for items which sell for $300 (£190/€265). For information about the practical application of this design, please see Katherine Newcomer's chapter "Exploring the Decision Making Process of the NetNeutral Platform".

What is Online Dispute Resolution?

As our different authors have made clear in their chapters, Online Dispute Resolution (ODR) represents a broad range of activities across a wide range of industries. An ODR system may be as simple as an email-based process for collecting documents. It could also be a process that uses highly sophisticated systems including data collection and storage, automated response processes, computer assisted resolution, internet supported conferencing, and a multitude of other services.

Definitions

Online Dispute Resolution

As early as 2002 the American Bar Association (ABA) Task Force on Electronic Commerce and Alternative Dispute Resolution Final Report provided this definition:

"Online Dispute Resolution (ODR) uses alternative dispute resolution processes to resolve a claim or dispute. Online Dispute Resolution can be used for disputes arising from an online, e-commerce transaction, or disputes arising from an issue not involving the Internet, called an "offline" dispute.

Dispute Resolution is an alternative to the traditional legal process, which usually involves a court, judge, and possibly a jury to decide the dispute.

Online Dispute Resolution can involve the parties in mediation, arbitration, and negotiation. The parties may use the Internet and web-based technology in a variety of ways. Online Dispute Resolution can be done entirely on the Internet, or "online," through email, videoconferencing, or both. The parties can also meet in person, or "offline. Sometimes, combinations of "online" and "off-line" methods are used in Online Dispute Resolution. ODR may be used, of course, to resolve disputes generated online as well as offline."

E-commerce companies often provide ODR as a service to customers. ODR forms a critical part of their customer retention and customer recovery strategies.

Traditional companies also use ODR in settling disputes regarding insurance claims, labour union and human resource issues as well as contractual issues. The ABA Task Force cited offered this list:

"ODR, as a process, may involve various types of dispute resolution including:

- dispute prevention (education, outreach, rating and feedback programmes);

- ombudsman programmes;

- conflict management;

- assisted negotiation;

- early neutral evaluation and assessment;

- mediation/conciliation;

- mediation-arbitration (binding and/or non-binding);

- arbitration;

- expert determination;

- executive tribunals; and

- consumer programmes (private, trade groups, quasi-governmental, and governmental)."

Mediation

Mediation is an effective way of resolving disputes. An independent third party, a Mediator, helps both sides come to an agreement. The Mediator serves as a facilitator and assists the parties in finding a solution to the problem that both parties can accept.

Mediators are responsible for developing effective communications and building consensus between the parties. The focus of a mediation meeting is to reach a common sense settlement. Mediators do not take sides, advocate for a position, make judgements or give guidance.

Mediation is a considered a confidential process. It is voluntary process and will only take place if both parties agree.

Arbitration

Arbitration is a process used to resolve disputes outside the courts. The parties to a dispute agree to send it to arbitration and agree to be bound by the arbitration decision (the "award"). A third, the Neutral, reviews the evidence in the case and makes a decision that is legally binding on both sides and enforceable in the courts.

In some countries arbitration is considered part of the legal, or court system, and therefore is not considered to be Alternative Dispute Resolution (ADR). In those cases, a similar process, called Adjudication, may be available.

Adjudication

Adjudication is a process in which an arbiter or judge reviews evidence and arguments including legal reasoning presented opposing parties, and then reaches a decision which determines rights and obligations between the parties involved.

With all of these ADR processes the third party may be a single neutral or may be a panel of neutrals.

Choosing a Process

Deciding which system has the potential to fit a company's particular needs is not complicated, but it does take a bit of time, some basic research, and a thorough discussion of the requirements of the parties in dispute.

Basically, ODR is a good option for any dispute which can be easily documented. The documentation can be provided as text or in the form of digital information which can be uploaded, such as photos, videos or scanned documents.

As an example, a typical ODR process that would be appropriate for disputes between traders and consumers could be based on the UNCITRAL Working Group III proposed rules for Online Dispute Resolution. See the Pablo Cortés chapter for more detail or http://www.uncitral.org/uncitral/commission/working_groups/3Online_Dispute_Resolution.html. Often these types of disputes fit in a category called "low value disputes", which generally involve business-consumer transactions with a financial value of less than £750 or €1000.

Disputes of this type can be handled completely online and would incorporate the following actions.

- Initial filing by the Claimant (usually the consumer)

- Notice to the Respondent (usually the trader)

- Providing explanation of how the process works

- Providing technical assistance, if needed, to the Claimant and the Respondent

- Appointing a qualified neutral party to serve as Mediator

- Collecting documentation and statements from the Claimant and Respondent

- Conducting a dialogue between the Claimant, the Respondent and the Mediator to find a mutually acceptable, fair settlement

- Preparation of the Proposed Settlement

- Collecting signatures/acceptance of the Settlement from the Claimant and Respondent

or

- Documenting the fact that the parties did not find an acceptable settlement; that the dispute ended in an impasse.

- In some instances, there may be also an Adjudication process, also completed online.

Main Advantages

The main advantages of this process are speed and convenience. The primary disadvantage is that the parties do not meet in person which has the potential to reduce their willingness to work through complicated issues and reach a mutually acceptable, fair settlement.

More complex issues, or higher value disputes, may also use ODR for collecting documents, for appointing the neutral party and for scheduling an in person meeting. For example, home repairs or home extensions often include an inspection of the property. In this way the Claimant, the Respondent and the Mediator can look at the current condition of the home and gather first-hand information. Automotive disputes and those involving professional services may also be better managed with an in person meeting.

The main advantages of this process are that it blends the efficiencies of online document collection with documents easily shared, viewed by both parties and the Mediator at any time, and the inclusion of an in-person inspection and meeting enables everyone to view the physical condition of the item in dispute. Meeting in person has also proved helpful in strengthening relationships. The primary disadvantage is the additional cost of the meeting and the additional Mediator's time.

ODR can be used for higher value business to business transactions. A typical example would include several schemes used in the US to settle insurance claims. Contractual issues and financial disputes between traders are also being resolved online.

Example of Business to Business ODR

For example, an online escrow payment company determined a robust dispute resolution process would offer reassurance to its clients. The company decided it would contract with a third party provider. Using an external scheme offers credibility, and it helps reduce the potential retaliation that might result from an unpopular decision. NetNeutrals discussed the needs of the online escrow company and helped define their goals for its ODR program.

The company offered an escrow payment service for commercial transactions. A typical transaction would be one where a buyer places an order with a new, unknown supplier. When the order is accepted, the buyer would place the funds in escrow with the online company. The supplier would fill the order and the buyer would have up to 10 days to let the supplier know if there were any problems. If no problems are reported the online company would release the escrowed funds to the supplier.

A Double Blind Settlement Scheme

In the event of a dispute and ODR process was created, which is called a Double Blind Settlement scheme. It allows both parties to file a position statement and to upload supporting documents. Time is of the essence due to the large value of the dispute. Consequently, the parties are allowed about one week to present their case. Each party is able to view and to comment on the documents submitted by the other side.

In addition, the parties are required to file a Proposed Settlement, which cannot be seen by the other side, which is why it is called Double Blind.

Once the position statements and the Proposed Settlements are filed, a third party (the Neutral) reviews the statements and the Proposed Settlements and decides the matter. It is assumed the Neutral will select one of the Proposed Settlements, which is expected to motivate both the buyer and the supplier to be reasonable in their expectations. The Neutral has the authority to adjust the terms in the interest of fairness or when there are legal requirements or other factors that must be considered. NetNeutrals committed to providing decision makers who are attorneys of qualified accountants. Final decision will be published within 24 hours of both parties posting positions and Proposed Settlements.

The primary advantage of this scheme is the speed and the qualifications of the Neutral, along with the fact that the online escrow company has the ability to immediately enforce the terms of the decision. The disadvantage, again, is that the parties do not have the opportunity to work through relationship issues once the process is started. It may be assumed that in many of these situations the parties have already determined they will terminate the business relationship.

In some countries ODR is used to handle family law cases, such as divorce and child custody issues. Others have developed ODR schemes to handle landlord-tenant issues. Canada uses ODR to settle property tax disputes between municipalities and home owners.

More Advantages of ODR

One of the main advantages of ODR is its speed. For example, the eBay IFR process takes 7 days.

There are numerous other benefits, such as the ability for the process to be managed asynchronously. In other words, the parties can log on at their convenience. These schemes eliminate the need to coordinate schedules and to arrange a physical meeting location.

The ABA Task Force on Electronic Commerce and Alternative Dispute Resolution report discussed earlier explains why ODR is a popular choice.

"Advantages of Online Dispute Resolution include:

- *Cost – Online Dispute Resolution is often less expensive than the traditional legal process*

- *Efficiency – Online Dispute Resolution can often resolve the dispute quickly*

- *Participation and Control – parties using Online Dispute Resolution must work with each other to resolve the dispute and often have more control of the outcome of the dispute.*

- *Flexibility – parties using Online Dispute Resolution can have more flexibility than the traditional legal process.*

- *Geographic flexibility – Online Dispute Resolution can allow parties in different locations or countries to avoid the costs and inconveniences of travel."*

Critical Credibility Considerations

When designing an ODR scheme, as with other design projects, attention to the details helps ensure a smooth launch and enhances the public's view of the programme.

The Global Business Dialogue on Electronic Commerce produced Alternative Dispute Resolution Guidelines in 2003.

See http://www.gbd-e.org/ig/cc/Alternative_Dispute_Resolution _Nov03.pdf

ODR is simply Alternative Dispute Resolution (ADR) accomplished online; therefore the guidelines are still sound considerations. The recommendations are excerpted here:

Impartiality

The ADR personnel must be impartial, in order to guarantee that decisions are recognized as being made independently, thus safeguarding the reputation and credibility of the organization providing ADR. Impartiality must be guaranteed by adequate arrangements. The governing structure of the ADR service should be designed so as to ensure neutrality in all respects.

Dispute resolution personnel must be insulated from pressure to favour merchants or consumers in resolving disputes. When the amount in dispute is large and/or when ADR is finally binding for both parties, even higher standards of transparency should be respected, including e.g. that the names of dispute resolution officers are made known to the parties, who should have the right to challenge them for cause. When a merchant uses a particular arbitration service repeatedly, to the extent practicable, the ADR officers who handle the disputes should be rotated to ensure their continued impartiality.

Qualification of ADR officers

Dispute resolution officers should have sufficient skills and training to fulfill the function in a satisfactory manner. Formal lawyer qualification and license should not be required.

Accessibility and Convenience

ADR systems must be easily accessible from each possible country. Online access might be the preferred choice. Requirements about the form of the submission of a case should be kept to the necessary minimum. Customers should receive maximum guidance in filling in and filing submissions. Appropriate solutions must also be found for any problems that may result from different languages used by the merchant, the ADR service provider and the customer.

Speed

To be effective, ADR systems must resolve disputes quickly if they are to meet the needs of both consumers and businesses. In any case, they must be speedier than courts in providing satisfactory results.

Low Cost for the Consumer

The ADR service should be provided to the consumer at no or only moderate cost, while taking into account the need to avoid frivolous claims. An impartial screening process provided by the ADR system could do this. Prior submission of a complaint to a customer satisfaction program will also permit an early assessment of the real nature of the claim.

In fact, the cost of ADR will be significantly lower for both consumers and businesses than formal administrative or legal actions.

Transparency

ADR systems should function according to published rules of procedure that describe unambiguously all relevant elements necessary to enable customers seeking redress to take fully informed decisions on whether they wish to use the ADR offered or address themselves to a court of law....

The ADR provider should publish an annual report enabling a meaningful evaluation of all ADR cases and results, while respecting the confidential nature of specific case information and data. Such evaluation should include – at a minimum - an aggregated list of cases received, cases settled prior to ADR resolution, cases settled by ADR resolution and cases not resolved.

To the degree possible, such report should include information on whether cases settled prior to, and at settlement, were to the advantage of the consumer or the merchant.

In cases where arbitration is binding on one or both of the parties, information should be available to the public about the identity of the merchant, the type of dispute, and to the degree possible, whether the dispute was resolved in favour of the merchant or the consumer.

Principle of Representation

The ADR procedure should not deprive the parties of the right to be represented or assisted by a third party at all stages of the procedure.

Applicable Rules

One of the principal reasons why business, consumers and governments consider the development of ADR systems to be of such strategic importance for the enhancement of consumer trust in electronic commerce is that such systems can settle disputes in an adequate fashion without necessarily engaging in cumbersome, costly, and difficult research on the detailed legal rules that would have to be applied in an official court procedure.

Governments in particular, must be confident that the rights of both consumers and businesses are protected, while at the same time avoiding actions that could adversely impact the growth of global electronic commerce.

ADR dispute resolution officers may decide in equity and/or on the basis of codes of conduct. This flexibility as regards the grounds for ADR decisions provides an opportunity for the development of high standards of consumer protection worldwide.

Consumer Awareness

Except in special cases where both consumers and merchants find special circumstances to agree to arbitration (see below), consumers will not alienate their right to go to court by electing to use an ADR mechanism.

ADR should be presented as a voluntary option for consumers if a dispute arises, not as a contractual obligation.

Decision Criteria

Each party to the dispute will need to know how their claims will be evaluated. In other words, what information is important and what is not pertinent. Helping the parties present a clear and compelling case helps ensure the Neutral is aware of all of the facts.

When the issues in dispute have a governing document, such as a contract or a warranty, of if there are legal or regulatory requirements, the parties can use that information as a guide for presenting their arguments.

In other situations, such as the eBay feedback disputes, there was no prior written set of expectations. While eBay had stated policies and procedures, it was necessary to collect and consolidate that data into a document that could be used by the parties and the decision maker. Historical information provided a list of the difficulties that Sellers experienced. The actual experiences were matched to the eBay policies which enabled NetNeutrals to develop Guidelines for Feedback Removal.

Sellers' experiences suggested the decision maker would need to know:

- Did both parties attempt to communicate directly and respond?

- How soon was the feedback left?

- Did the parties make an effort to take action?

- Did both parties allow the other a reasonable amount of time to remedy the concern?

- Did the item description include all pertinent information?

- Are any mechanical issues reasonable, given the age/mileage of the vehicle and product type?

- Has either party violated eBay's rules and policies?

- Are both parties' claims and expectations reasonable?

- Are both parties' claims supported with facts and specific reference?

Four Guidelines for Feedback Removal

NetNeutrals condensed this data and developed four Guidelines for Feedback Removal.

1. A good faith effort was made to complete the transaction

2. The feedback was left in a timely manner

3. There is a lack of evidence to suggest that the information contained in the feedback is factually inaccurate

4. There is a lack of evidence to suggest extortion of excessive value

Designing Guidelines for Feedback Removal helps both parties know what criteria the decision maker will be using. The parties are told at the beginning of the process that "clear and convincing evidence" must be presented. For detail on the practical application of these Guidelines see Katherine Newcomer's case by case discussion in her chapter "Online Dispute Resolution Decision Making – A NetNeutrals Practitioner's View".

How to Choose an ODR Provider

Many organizations will decide to develop an ODR process, but others will conclude they are better served by contracting with a professional ODR provider, or may be required by law to use an outside firm.

Here are some suggestions from the report on American Bar Association's Task Force on electronic Commerce which was cited previously.

"When considering Online Dispute Resolution Provider, consider the following:

- The qualifications of the neutral,

- Are the policies easily understood and found quickly?

- Is the Online Dispute Resolution Provider impartial, having no relationship with either party?

- Make sure you know the physical location, address, and phone number of the Online Dispute Resolution Provider.

- Is the Online Dispute Resolution accessible regarding different languages and accommodations for parties with disabilities?

- Is the confidentiality policy clear and fair?

- Is the cost less than traditional litigation methods?"

Key Points

1. Estimates show there will be one billion online disputes by 2017.

2. ODR is a rapidly growing field, with established procedures and recommended best practices. ODR offer quick, efficient and effective systems for finding fair resolutions across a wide range of industries and types of disputes.

3. ODR offers sensible solutions to increasing customer satisfaction. ODR can be an effective tool for recovering customers and positively impacting customer recommendations.

4. Employing appropriate systems in the design on an ODR scheme will positively impact the reputation of the scheme and of the company who offers it.

5. Independence and fairness are at the heart of all credible ODR schemes.

Online Dispute Resolution for Businesses – Embedding Online Dispute Resolution in the European Civil Justice System

Pablo Cortés

Senior Lecturer, School of Law, University of Leicester

Introduction

Digital technology is becoming an essential means of communication for most people. Increasingly, consumers are entering into contracts online, so inevitably more conflicts are arising from online transactions. However, court litigation for these disputes is nearly always inconvenient, time-consuming and expensive due to the low value of the transactions and the physical distance between the parties. Online Dispute Resolution (ODR) often referred as online access to forms of Alternative Dispute Resolution (ADR) such as negotiation, mediation, conciliation, arbitration, and ombudsman processes. ODR is the best (and often the only) option for enhancing the redress of consumer grievances, strengthening their trust in the market, and promoting the sustainable growth of e-commerce.

Online market places such as eBay have harnessed the power of ODR to increase trust and loyalty amongst its users. Indeed, eBay is a good case study for ODR. Whether it is through the dispute resolution centre of its main payment partner, PayPal, which resolves a staggering number of 60 million disputes a year, or through one of its trusted independent ODR providers, such as NetNeutrals for feedback disputes arising from car sales, ODR offers parties in disputes with an adequate forum for setting disputes. The chapters from Jo De Mars and Katherine Newcomer give more detail on how the approach works in practice. Although the application of ODR is not limited to disputes arising out of online transactions, it seems to be particularly apt for these disputes, since it is logical to use the same medium (the internet) for the resolution of e-commerce disputes. For that reason there is ongoing institutional effort from the UN and at the EU to enhance the use of ODR for resolving these types of disputes. An emerging regulatory framework intends to promote the participation of online users with contractual disputes in certified ODR schemes, providing them with more adequate and efficient redress options.

This chapter examines the two most important regulatory initiatives in the field of ODR: the draft procedural rules of the UN Commission for International Trade Law (UNCITRAL) Working Group III on ODR for cross-border low-value electronic commerce transactions; and the two legal instruments on consumer ADR and ODR in the EU i.e. Directive 2013/11/EU on Alternative Dispute Resolution for Consumer Disputes and Regulation (EC) 524/2013 on Online Dispute Resolution for Consumer Disputes. These legal norms incorporate recognised best practices into ODR processes, and in doing so, they have started a process of professionalising a traditionally unregulated sector. The rationale behind this regulatory effort is the promotion of ODR as the primary form of dispute resolution for many disputes, especially those arising from e-commerce and consumer transactions. This institutionalisation process is therefore moving ODR systems from the unregulated models of redress to an increasingly important part of the civil justice system in the United Kingdom and the rest of Europe.

International Efforts to Regulate and Promote ODR by the United Nations Commission for International Trade Law

The function of UNCITRAL is to help make international trade law more compatible in order to enhance cross-border trade. With this goal in mind, the UNCITRAL has established a Working Group to develop a legal framework in the field of ODR related to cross-border transactions. In December 2010 UNCITRAL Working Group III commenced to prepare draft procedural rules (hereinafter "the rules") that may serve as a model for ODR providers that deal with commercial and consumer cross-border low-value, high-volume disputes arising from e-commerce. The outcome of the Group's work will be, it is hoped, model contractual dispute resolution terms, akin to the INCOTERMS developed by the ICC for international trade, which parties may include when entering into online transactions.

UNCITRAL draft ODR rules

Scope of application

The rules are being drafted for the resolution of disputes arising from cross-border low-value, high-volume transactions conducted by means of electronic communications. The rules will only apply to claims related to goods sold which were not delivered, not timely delivered, not properly charged in accordance with the contract. Hence, it will exclude claims such as consequential damage or personal injury. The language of the proceedings will be the language agreed by the parties, or, in defect of such agreement, in the language chosen by the neutral third party. The automated part of the ODR process, i.e. the negotiation stage, is expected to be multi-lingual and parties will be able to use software to translate texts.

Multi-Step ODR Process

The rules establish an ODR process in stages (including negotiation, facilitation, and arbitration/recommendation) to be agreed between the parties that have entered into the transaction now in dispute. The Working Group decided that the rules should offer two distinct sets of procedures: Track I ending in binding arbitration, and Track II finishing in a recommendation which may be enforceable via private mechanisms, such as a trustmark scheme. The two track system displays the different approaches held in various jurisdictions, where according to many national laws, particularly the USA, pre-dispute arbitration clauses are allowed; while national laws in other jurisdictions, such as the EU Member States, Japan, and many Latin American countries invalidate these clauses in consumer contracts.

Both tracks start with an online negotiation where parties will use the framework provided by the software. This is often referred to as assisted or facilitated negotiation. Parties will negotiate through the standard forms provided by the ODR system to facilitate communications during the negotiation, for example, by contacting the other party or by identifying and clarifying important information.

When parties cannot reach an agreement in the negotiation stage, the ODR provider will select a neutral third party who will act, depending on the track chosen by the parties, as an arbitrator (Track I) and when necessary as facilitator as well, or as an evaluator making a non-legally binding recommendation (Track II).

In Track I the rules provide that the arbitrator will resolve the claim within 15 days after the parties have submitted all the required documents. The arbitral award will be final and binding on the parties. In Track II, the neutral will issue a non-binding recommendation, which, although it will not be enforceable in courts (i.e. it will not have *res judicata* effect), may be enforced through private mechanisms.

Regardless whether binding or non-binding arbitration is employed, the implementation of the process will likely be coupled with sufficient incentives to promote parties' rapid and voluntary compliance with the outcomes. There are a number of incentives that may be used to encourage voluntary compliance with a settlement: rating systems (e.g. feedback models like eBay's); publication of awards, especially when one of the parties had not complied with the outcome (black list); trustmark logo that may be withdrawn when the vendor had not complied with the award; communicating the outcome to a consumer agency or the relevant public authority in the nation of the respondent or co-operation with search engines which may give a lower ranking to those who refuse to comply with outcomes. The issues around enforcement are considered in more detail in the chapter by Riika Koulu.

The regional efforts in the EU to promote ODR

This section examines the key provisions of this new European legal framework which aims to increase the availability of high quality ADR schemes as well as to encourage their use. By July 2015 all EU Member States must have complied with the requirements set in the ADR Directive, which main obligation requires EU Member States to ensure the provision and availability of ADR schemes that comply with minimum legal standards when resolving disputes between traders and consumers. Participation by businesses in ADR will remain voluntary in most economic sectors, but businesses must inform consumers about certified ADR schemes. The ODR Regulation mandates the European Commission to establish a pan-European ODR Platform that will become a single point of entry for resolving online consumer complaints arising from e-commerce. The platform, which is fully operational from January 2016, links complainants to nationally certified ADR schemes.

Directive on alternative dispute resolution for consumers

Scope of application

The ADR Directive imposes an obligation on the EU Members States to ensure the provision of out-of-court settlement mechanisms, accessible online, for consumer complaints. The Directive thus requires Member States to ensure the provision of certified ADR schemes for the resolution of domestic and cross-border consumer complaints, arising from the sale of goods and the provision of services. Member States may meet this obligation by either ensuring that there are private or public certified ADR schemes in all economic sectors, or by setting at least one residual certified ADR scheme that operates in all the sectors where there is not already an ADR scheme. Yet, importantly, the Directive does not make the use of ADR mandatory in any economic sector, nor does it affect the existing national laws that oblige traders in their specific sectors to participate in ADR schemes.

The scope of the ADR Directive covers consumer (but not trader) complaints arising from contracts of sales and services, both offline and online, including the provision of digital content for remuneration.

Member States must thus guarantee the availability of quality ADR schemes where consumers are complainants. The Directive covers both, binding and non-binding ADR processes, and it describes ADR schemes as adjudicative and consensual extrajudicial schemes created on a durable basis. Furthermore, Member States can decide whether the ADR schemes established on their territories have the power to impose a decision –in other words, a Member State may limit the accreditation to consensual ADR schemes, restricting the use of arbitration schemes (but it cannot restrict the operation of a consumer arbitration scheme established in another Member State that offers its services in a Member State which does not certify arbitration schemes).

Certified ADR schemes will have a competitive advantage as they will be subject to higher standards than those that are not certified, so consumers and businesses are likely to choose certified schemes. Non-accredited ADR schemes dealing with e-commerce disputes will find themselves at a commercial disadvantage because they would not be included in the ODR platform. Also, businesses and consumers will be signposted towards certified ADR schemes, even when businesses have chosen to participate in a non-certified ADR scheme.

Certified ADR Bodies

Certified ADR schemes must accept both domestic and cross-border disputes, including those referred by the European ODR platform. This requirement however does not imply that certified ADR schemes will be required to offer their services in all the European languages. Certified ADR schemes dealing with e-commerce disputes must provide a link in their website to the EU ODR platform, and the scheme may, but it is not required to, conduct the ADR procedure relating to a dispute it has received via the ODR platform using the case management tool provided in the EU ODR platform.

In any event, the ADR procedure must be available online and offline. These ADR schemes must have a website which allows parties to access information about the ADR procedure, to submit complaints and supporting documents online. Complaints referred by the ODR platform will be resolved online, unless both the ADR scheme and the parties agreed to an offline process. Parties cannot be required to have legal representation, though they can have it if they so choose. Parties may also be able to request information on a durable medium (i.e. on paper or via email) and submit a complaint offline, if that is what the consumer chooses, in what would be exceptional circumstances. The ADR procedure must be free or available at a nominal cost to the consumer and must comply with data protection legislation.

While certified ADR schemes can, and often do, specialise in economic sectors or types of disputes, e.g. complaints against energy or telecom providers, they cannot refuse complaints arbitrarily. The refusal must be reasoned and communicated to the complainant within three weeks of receiving the complete complaint file. Neutral third parties must have adequate expertise, be impartial and have no conflict of interest and collegial bodies must have equal stakeholder representation for consumers and traders. Neutrals do not have to be licensed legal practitioners, but they must have the necessary knowledge in the field of ADR or judicial resolution of consumer disputes, and a general understanding of law.

The Directive sets a number of information requirements that ADR schemes must make available on their websites and provided in a durable medium if requested by one of the parties. In addition, certified ADR schemes will have to publish on their websites an annual activity report. ADR processes must be free-of-charge or at moderate cost to consumers, regardless of the value of the complaint; and ADR schemes will decide in three weeks from the submission of the complaint whether they are competent to deal with a dispute; in that case the complaint should be resolved within 90 days of its submission. If one compares the length of time taken by successful ODR providers such as eBay's Resolution Centre, then it appears clear that the ideal time frame for resolving low-value disputes should be shorter, ideally less than a week.

Information obligations for businesses

Traders have to inform consumers if they have voluntarily become affiliated with a particular certified ADR scheme or if they are required to participate in ADR processes by law or by industry as part of the membership to a particular trade association. Examples of regulated sectors where the provision of ADR is often mandatory are the financial sector and some utility providers such as gas and electricity and telecoms. When the trader is part of an ADR scheme it must provide the information in its website and in the Terms and Conditions of sales or service contracts. Interestingly, a number of Member States, such as Germany and Slovenia, have extended this obligation by requiring all those traders who are not committed to use ADR, to put an express statement of their decision (that they are not committed to participate in an ADR process) in their Terms and Conditions, in both the paper format and on their websites.

In addition, all businesses operating online must include a link in their website to the ODR platform. This obligation is extended to those websites that act as intermediaries between sellers and buyers –well known examples of these online market places are eBay and Amazon.

There is also another information obligation that kicks in every time a trader has an unresolved dispute with a consumer. In these cases the trader is required to notify consumers about the certified ADR schemes operating in the sector, and clearly inform the consumer whether or not the trader uses any of the ADR schemes to settle the dispute. Although, it appears a bit strange that traders are legally required to inform consumers of ADR schemes, even when they have no intention of using them, this obligation was included because it is believed that it will encourage traders to refer disputes to ADR schemes by forcing them to consider in every case whether ADR is appropriate.

Regulation (EC) 524/2013 on online dispute resolution

ADR processes in the consumer sector, especially in the cross-border and e-commerce context, cannot be promoted without the relevant technological support. The role of technology in these online processes is so fundamental that it has been labelled as the 'fourth party' because it displaces, and sometimes replaces, the role of the neutral third party. The European Commission has realized that ADR processes for consumers should be complemented with technology. This conclusion led to the approval of the ODR Regulation as a complement to the ADR Directive. The ODR Regulation ensures the accessibility of ADR processes through an ODR platform that offers a means of distance communication between the parties and ADR schemes. It is to this Regulation that we turn now.

Scope of application

The ODR Regulation establishes a EU-wide ODR platform that aims to facilitate the resolution of consumer disputes, domestic and cross-border, arising from e-commerce. If the ODR platform becomes successful in resolving e-commerce disputes, it will surely lead to the expansion to other sectors, or even to all types of consumer disputes. Currently, the main limitation of the EU ODR platform is that it does not have a system of automatic referral to an ADR scheme if the business does not reply to the consumer's claim.

The ODR platform

The ODR platform, which is accessible through Your Europe Portal – http://europa.eu/youreurope/citizens/index_en.htm - offers consumers a single point of entry to resolve domestic and cross-border complaints arising from e-commerce. Certified ADR schemes competent to deal with these disputes will be registered in the ODR platform. Moreover, at the time of writing, fifteen EU Member States have already developed online portals or helpdesks, which, like the EU ODR platform, act as clearinghouses signposting complainants to nationally approved ADR schemes. The features of these portals vary, but they can be also connected to the EU ODR platform provided they develop this functionality.

The platform's main role is therefore to transfer the complaint from the complainant to the defendant in a European language chosen by the defendant. It will also assist the parties in identifying a competent ADR scheme and enable them to exchange information online through the platform. Yet, if parties do not agree on participating in an ADR process within 30 days, then the complaint will be dismissed. It is at this point when the ODR contact point through its two ODR advisors should notify the complainant about mandatory ADR schemes, if there is one, or, in its absence, with information on other means of redress, such as the availability of a small claims procedure.

Conclusion

The goal of these two legal initiatives, the UNCITRAL rules and EU's legislation, is the stimulation of trade, in particular the digital dimension of cross-border trade. In order to achieve this goal they are developing a regulatory framework with the hope of installing greater confidence in e-commerce. The new framework aims to promote the use of ODR by giving market visibility (through an accreditation process) to ODR providers that comply with rules of due process. While both initiatives envisage an accreditation system, the European system takes consumer ODR a step further by requiring Member States to ensure the provision of ADR/ODR schemes in compliance with the procedural guarantees established in the ADR Directive. Furthermore, whereas UNCITRAL proposes a multi-step procedure that moves from online negotiation up to adjudication/recommendation, the European consumer ODR initiative encompasses all types of ADR/ODR processes, leaving the establishment of specific procedures to the individual ADR/ODR schemes. The UNCITRAL and EU initiatives thus complement each other, as EU consumers may be offered an ODR process that follows the UNCITRAL rules.

Policymakers are setting up the infrastructure to promote the use of ADR/ODR schemes, especially for consumer and low value disputes. In the EU, quality ADR/ODR schemes can already undergo a public certification system and traders have the legal obligation to notify consumers with unresolved complaints about these certified schemes. This is an important change in the civil justice system which no longer sees the courts as the default forum to resolve these types of disputes. Although currently it is voluntary for most traders to opt into these schemes, the day when the participation in certified ADR/ODR schemes becomes mandatory as the primary forum for resolving these disputes is not far away. In the meantime businesses that value customer care will seize the opportunity and embrace ADR/ODR voluntarily to demonstrate the quality of their products and services as well as their willingness to treat customers fairly.

Take Away Points

- Technology is permeating our lives, including our buying and selling habits. It is now the time to harness its potential to facilitate the resolution of disputes, especially to settle those arising from an online forum.

- The new EU regulatory framework and the UNCITRAL draft ODR rules aim to increase the awareness and the participation in ADR/ODR processes, increasing access to justice in economic sectors where there is limited access to redress. It is believed that a greater use of ODR will strengthen consumer trust in e-commerce; especially, but not exclusively, in cross-border trade.

- Best practices for out-of-court dispute resolution are now enshrined in legal rules that require EU Member States to certify quality ADR/ODR schemes.

- All traders with unresolved disputes now have the legal obligation to notify consumers about certified ADR/ODR schemes. Therefore, ADR/ODR schemes are now imbedded firmly as a pillar of our civil justice system, which no longer relies on the public courts as the default channel for settling consumer issues.

Consumer Trust and Business Benefits with ODR

Immaculada Barral-Viñals

Professor of Private Law, University of Barcelona; Salvador de Madariaga Fellow at the Cyberjustice Laboratory, Centre de Recherche en Droit Public (Public Law Research Centre), University of Montreal

Case study – Lack of Trust

We can easily imagine the situation where a number of years ago, *Arnaud et fils*, a small French firm dealing in electronic consumer goods, spent a small fortune in setting up their own interactive website. If France's national statistics are anything to go by, the amount of business being conducted in other European countries is astonishingly low. Nonetheless our consumer, Olga Marconi an Italian resident visits the firm's website and finds an attractive price for an accessory for her iPad. Yet the fact that it is a foreign company made her stop short of placing her order for fear that if the accessory was never sent or if it turned out to be faulty, the problems she would face resolving the dispute would be insurmountable.

Consumers Hold Back

The recent Digital Single Market Strategy for Europe reports some revealing statistics: 61% of EU consumers feel confident about purchasing via the Internet from a retailer/provider located in their own country, but only 38% feel confident about purchasing via Internet from a vendor in another EU Member State, while only 7% of SMEs in the EU sell cross-border.

Across the European Union, there are more than 500 million potential consumers of goods and services, and the existence of the EU's internal market places this opportunity well within the reach of Europe's producers, including its small and medium-sized enterprises (SMEs). That this trade can be conducted online makes the potential turnover of this business even more attractive. Indeed, after the introduction of the Euro, the online market could have become the second main factor in promoting this internal market. So why has this not yet become a reality even with the EU's long-standing commitment to the development of e-commerce as a growth factor? Is it because the problems associated with getting redress for a problem with a cross-border transaction have deterred both consumers and businesses from committing themselves fully. What are these problems?

Legal Fragmentation

The first problem encountered is determining which laws and jurisdiction should be applied. Although many aspects of consumer protection law have been harmonized, Pablo Cortés writes that the legal fragmentation represented by the EU-27 countries makes knowing the law applicable to each contract a complicated task for the parties to the dispute. Yet, confidence in the online environment does not depend solely on legislative harmonization (although it is an issue that clearly needs to be tackled). E-confidence also depends on a responsive system of conflict resolution, more so perhaps than in traditional 'over the counter' local relationships. Only when individual redress is accessible, swift and cheap, can consumers feel comfortable with transactions of this type. For this reason, consumers need a straightforward, inexpensive system for seeking redress and only when this can be guaranteed will consumers run the risk of default or defective performance on the part of the firm.

Business Impact

Businesses face similar needs. Indeed, having a good understanding of consumer complaint systems and the costs that they incur for them is essential. However, businesses need to be aware not only of the direct costs – that is, the fees charged for using a dispute resolution service (which on occasions are in fact free) - but also of the indirect costs, including the impact of delayed or cancelled payments, as well as staffing costs incurred in dealing with complaints whether accepted or rejected. Finally, companies must consider the impact of any disputes on a brand's image as well as on the return on past investment in consumer trust.

EU System by 2016

To address this situation, the Digital Single Market Strategy is focused on overcoming the legal obstacles to the development of e-commerce in the internal market, with regards both to reforming the legal framework and to creating appropriate processes of dispute resolution that can be swift, flexible and effective. One of the means for achieving this is the establishment of an EU-wide online dispute resolution (ODR) platform, which will be operational from July 2016.

From ADR to ODR in Consumer Disputes

In 1993, the EU opted to channel the resolution of consumer complaints through processes of alternative dispute resolution (ADR) as stated in the Green Paper on access of consumers to justice. ADR offers highly varied schemes from a legal point of view comprising systems of negotiation, mediation, arbitration and ombudsmen. According to the EU, there are currently more than 750 ADR schemes in the Union, although only 462 (60%) appear in their databases. So, currently, not all ADR schemes meet the legal requisites laid down by the EU for registration as systems of ADR and this indicates that a process of homogenization is needed. Directive 2013/11/EU on alternative dispute resolution for consumer disputes (hereinafter, DADR) creates a system of accreditation of national ADR entities where the Member States have to determine whether the systems meet the requirements of transparency, independence, impartiality and legality to become accredited ADR entities. If they do, they may become part of the EU online platform.

ODR: The Need for Development in Consumer Disputes

In addition to the ADR schemes, since 2001 the EU has been aware that the use of ICT (Information and Communications Technology) in consumer dispute resolution constitutes an effective weapon for generating confidence in cross-border trade. From this date, recourse to ODR has become a leading strategy in consumer policy in the EU market, culminating in the Digital Single Market Strategy.

There are two reasons for this:

- The technical possibilities currently available for application in the field of conflict resolution

- The characteristics of consumer complaints that make them particularly suited to ODR systems

Technological Possibilities in Conflict Resolution

The search for efficiency, along with reduced costs, has meant that traditional ADR processes (an area where much experience has been gained) have been adapted for use online. The use of ICTs in conflict resolution occurs at a variety of levels from the use of ICT tools in court or in ADR schemes, thanks to the ease with which they can create new and better systems for resolving disputes. Indeed, ODRs employ a broad variety of tools that offer many different levels of interaction between these technical tools and the processes for resolving disputes. This versatility is based primarily on Web 2.0 and Web 3.0 technologies which offer real opportunities for developing the three main areas with which ODR is concerned: namely, communication, collaboration and interactivity. Nevertheless, the use of ICTs for conflict resolution is still limited, especially for consumer disputes, where the full range of interactions made possible by Web 2.0 and Web 3.0 remain at an embryonic stage. Nevertheless some progress has been made. For our purposes here, I have identified four different levels of ODR application:

1. The adaptation of traditional ADR processes to the new environment: foremost in this group are methods of e-arbitration or e-mediation where software development can design online arbitration or mediation procedures using techniques such as email, forums and videoconferencing.

2. The versatility of new technology means that mediation and negotiation procedures can be offered together online. The emphasis here is on the technical means for developing dialogue between the parties rather than on the intervention of a third party. The first step is normally a negotiation process, but if no result is obtained, the next step is to assign a mediator. In this environment, ODRs therefore tend to offer technological platforms for dialogue between the parties – with or without the intervention of a third party –with an opportunity for managed escalation procedures. A best-in-class example would be the platform for on-line litigants developed at the University of Montreal. - Plateforme d'Aide au Règlement des Litiges En ligne (PARLe).

3. New ODR capabilities: this is the real proof of what new technology can do when applied to conflict management on the web. In this case technology is used to the fullest, right from the outset, to design a process equivalent to a traditional ADR one. Amongst their most exciting possibilities are the "automatic negotiation systems" i.e. procedures carried out without human intervention. This is the great ODR innovation. These automated tools are used especially in monetary claims where the only matter in dispute is the amount of compensation the consumer should receive. This involves providing the necessary software to enable the parties to submit offers without knowing the amounts offered by the other party to the dispute. When the offers from both parties reach a certain percentage ratio, agreement is established automatically at the average of both. As can be imagined, this system is extremely swift and inexpensive, although the lack of human intervention may mean that some of the decisions are not optimal. Nevertheless, it remains a

prime example of the connection between new technology and online dispute resolution.

4. Future developments in ODR are linked to the use of artificial intelligence that can offer many possibilities of solving disputes. One is the case-based reasoning, where previous experience is used to analyse or solve new problems automatically. Another very important development is 'machine learning', where the artificial intelligence system attempts to gain new knowledge from an analysis of past cases. In this field of artificial intelligence, a lot of technical possibilities remain unexplored.

Consumer Conflicts Well-suited to ODR

Beyond the generation of e-confidence (see discussion above), there is a second reason that links consumer complaints to the use of electronic media; namely, the fact that the characteristics of such complaints make them especially suited to being resolved online. Indeed, the categorization provided in Chapter 5 of the White Book of Mediation in Catalonia, dedicated to mediation in the field of consumer complaints, identifies the general characteristics of these complaints and the applicability of ODR techniques. Among these characteristics, the following should be highlighted:

- The common situation whereby we see complaints with similar causes concentrated in a few sectors. This is associated with the phenomenon of the mass market where a consumer's ability to influence the content of a contract is very small. The general terms and conditions governing the sale of goods and services are very similar leading unsurprisingly to very similar sorts of disputes prompted by particular types of contract or commercial practice.

- The system is particularly suited to the low value of most disputes, which is in turn, an incentive to keep the costs of the process as low as possible. Indeed, most disputes do not involve very large sums. This point should not be overlooked given that the low value of most disputes is often out of all proportion to the costs of the potential litigation and the price of the product or service acquired. Thus, consumers are usually anxious to avoid having to go to court to settle the dispute, as is highlighted time and again in studies conducted in the EU. In fact, the use of alternative dispute resolutions for these disputes is not an "alternative", but rather they solve a set of problems that otherwise would remain unresolved.

- The existence of a typical system of distance mediation using electronic means: consumer mediation is not usually conducted in person, but is characterised by the use of e-mail correspondence in the communication between the parties mainly addressed to the mediator, although little use is made of interactive technology. In short, non face-to-face mediation is the norm.

These three characteristics make ODR schemes particularly appropriate for application to consumer complaints.

In short, the technical possibilities available, together with the characteristics of consumer complaints, make the development of ODR particularly relevant for this field. It is our belief that automatic or assisted schemes of negotiation, or hybrid systems of negotiation plus mediation and ombudsmen, can offer businesses a very attractive and cheap channel for attracting customers concerned about the problems of making cross-border transactions. Moreover, the DADR provides for the existence of dispute resolution schemes – as well as for ODR – in the context of private firms, although with additional guarantees of independence and transparency, if the Member States so authorize. Therefore, the possibilities exist to turn to an already existing public or private system or to promote the creation of a private system for businesses dedicated to conflict resolution in a given market sector, be it insurance or online retail purchases.

The European Platform of Online Conflict Resolution

The EU, as mentioned, is committed to creating a platform for general ODR that can be applied across all EU countries, by using accredited ADR entities. The platform is designed under Regulation 524/2013 of the European Parliament and the Council of 21 May 2013 on online dispute resolution (hereinafter, RODR) which can exploit ICT in resolving such disputes.

RODR provides for a "Network of ODR contact points" where each Member State's contact point is responsible for receiving complaints from consumers and for directing them to the competent entity for resolution. The network is an example of case management, relying on the existing centres in the Consumer Centres Network, as specifically stated under EU law. The second main innovation was the establishment of the ODR platform to be developed, operated and maintained by the Commission. This ODR is a case management platform functioning as an electronic gateway to an interactive Internet site via a "single point of entry"

The platform will be comprised of four main technical tools:

- an electronic complaint form;

- a translation system that does not rely solely on automated translation tools;

- a case management tool to identify the competent ADR entity to conduct the dispute resolution procedure; and

- a system providing general information about consumer rights and details about competent ADRs and ODR contact points, as well as guidelines for submitting complaints through the platform.

Initially, the platform is designed only to channel claims to the national competent authority and to serve as a reference point for communication between the parties during the process. Thus, it would serve as a 'meeting point' for the consumer and the ADR entity, pointing the complainant to the right resolution system. At this initial stage, the ODR tool is merely redirecting the complainant. The eventual resolution mechanism will be the competent and registered ADR system, as defined in the EU Directive whether it be mediation, arbitration or an Ombudsman's Office.

In short, the EU's ODR platform's main contribution is to channel the complaints to the competent resolution entity, by providing access to the system for a large number of low-value cross-border disputes. Indeed, redirecting the consumer complaint to the competent entity to resolve cross-border disputes can be considered the first step in encouraging consumers to enforce their rights in terms of the Digital Single Market Strategy. In this way, the platform will promote a resolution which in other circumstances would not be possible. Yet, the opportunity to use interactive tools for conflict resolution, which is technically feasible, appears to have been lost for the time being. The combination of a channelling tool and a case resolution system would have been highly positive for consumer redress. As things stand presently, the complainant has not only to identify a competent entity, but also deal with the problems presented by each ADR. This may well lead to a delay in getting the complaint resolved.

Even in this context, the platform represents a great opportunity for firms since it offers consumers the possibility of obtaining satisfaction via a straightforward, easy-to-use process (i.e., filling in a form online without having to leave the house). Moreover, it may well convince many consumers that the default risk can be minimized, as there is a real possibility of obtaining redress. Additionally, the system is even easier for business owners to use as all they have to do is join the competent dispute resolution scheme in their Member State and provide information about the platform on their website. This allows them to project an image of trust and to minimise the costs of managing complaints. However, it cannot be denied that the limited technical possibilities explored to-date might well lead to a delay in the management of the complaint.

Summary

- Some 500 million potential consumers in the EU express a certain degree of reluctance to buy online because of the risks of default or defective performance, especially in the case of transactions in another country.

- Mindful of this, the EU has committed itself to addressing such conflicts using the many ADR schemes now in operation across Europe, and adapting them to online processes, making resolution swifter and cheaper.

- Its most recent efforts have taken the shape of a platform for conflict resolution that directs each consumer complaint to the competent national ADR entity for its subsequent resolution. Although this has the potential of generating the e-confidence needed, it is apparent that limited exploitation of the possibilities provided by ICT to the resolution of disputes may compromise the chances of the platform's success.

- In fact, technology is available now for ODR schemes which not only facilitates the application of case management tools, such as the platform mentioned previously, but is also able to provide systems that do not require human intervention (automatic negotiation), managed escalated processes (negotiation through mediation up to an Ombudsman) and smart schemes based on artificial intelligence.

- Firms can opt to join their Member State's ADR entity which, from 2016 onwards, will be connected to the EU platform; or, alternatively, they can opt to use different models of private ODR schemes, where we can anticipate the emergence of sectoral systems.

- Whatever option is chosen, the provision of methods of conflict resolution using the most modern ICT technology would appear to offer undeniable advantages for all parties.

Where Law, Technology, Theory and Practice Overlap: Enforcement Mechanisms and System Design

Riikka Koulu, LL.M.,

Doctoral Candidate in Procedural Law, University of Helsinki

Why Enforcement Matters in ODR

Online Dispute Resolution (ODR) is a dynamic field of dispute resolution, where law and technology, theory and practice overlap. Providing an ODR option to business and their customers that delivers redress quickly and at low cost will increase consumer confidence for example in cross-border trade by helping to bypass the complexities and costs of unfamiliar legal systems.

Definition Deficit

Unfortunately, a comprehensive definition of ODR (Online Dispute Resolution) is still lacking. See Jo De Mars' chapter for a range of definitions as suggested in the US. This is at least partly explained by the diversity of tools needed when applying technology to dispute resolution. We can make a distinction between private ODR and courtroom technology, or discuss dispute resolution and technology as an umbrella term for both private and public conflict management. We can include facilitating technology e.g. case management systems, videoconferencing etc. in the definition, or maintain that only completely automated online procedures deserve the title of ODR. In literature, ODR has mostly been discussed in relation to e-commerce cases, i.e. low-value, high volume disputes arising from online transactions. However, ODR is being applied to more and more diverse case types, such as family law cases, and is no longer confined to its best-known application: e-commerce. The Laboratory of Cyberjustice of University of Montreal uses the terminology of 'low intensity disputes' to describe the characteristics of disputes that would be suitable for ODR. The terminology captures the essential characteristics of the dispute and the issues at stake for the parties without labelling them simply as e-commerce disputes. We also ask whether the definition of ODR should include courtroom application of technology, as well as the dispute resolution systems of e-commerce platforms, and conflict management of consumer relations in businesses.

Bringing technology to dispute resolution has been seen to provide efficient, and most importantly, fast access to resolution procedures. These effects become even more pronounced in cross-border cases, where the high costs of litigation often render redress through courts impossible.

Designing a Dispute Resolution System

Designing a dispute resolution system is a delicate interplay between several interest groups. The most important of these is the actual buyer of the software, who might be a company, public court, an e-commerce site or a private concern servicing a particular client or market sector. The needs of the buyer, whose interests vary depending on their conflict environment and the type of disputes, are the essential starting point for designing dispute resolution systems. The buyer's desired outcome is further elaborated into a more detailed process whereby lawyers define the relevant regulatory framework and define the necessary system characteristics from their perspective. The work of lawyers identifies the possibilities and limitations that follow from national legislation, cross-border legal instruments if applicable, case-law and fundamental human rights. After these starting points of process design, there is still a leap to actual software requirements, finding suppliers and defining contract details. The perspectives of conflict management and those of software programming need to be reconciled: in the end, the programmers are responsible for turning the legal specifications into actual technological infrastructure. The end product, completely or partly automated dispute resolution software for managing conflicts in online and offline worlds, is the result of a complicated multi-stepped process. Understanding this complexity of designing ODR systems is essential.

Problematic Process

Process definitions are by nature problematic, as they need to be understandable to both buyer and the supplier. What is more, the time span of a dispute resolved through ODR software does not end when the decision is rendered. For the disputing parties the dispute resolution process is ultimately an issue of forcing your legal position on the other - to recover owed money, to get a replacement product. Ultimately, the dispute can be considered as being at an end when the decision is put into practice, voluntarily or by resorting to some means of enforcement.

Enforcement in the ODR Era

Traditionally, courts and arbitral tribunals have rendered decisions, which are then enforced by the designated authorities. However, in the ODR era enforcement becomes a part of the system design in a different way than before. In particular, cross-border ODR solutions can seldom rely completely on official enforcement systems, because before a national authority collects a debt, they need a decision to proceed from either from a national court system or other specific requirements which have to be satisfied. In order to comply with such requirements or to find other alternatives for voluntary compliance with the ODR decision, enforcement has to be thought of as a part of the complete process design that is supra-national. Otherwise the ODR system faces the risk of not being effective enough to provide complete and final resolution of a dispute, thus failing to fulfil its promise of efficiency.

What Alternatives Are There?

Enforcement through National Courts

As stated, enforcement through its own courts has traditionally been the method for enforcing a decision in a specific nation state. This approach to enforcement through a state's monopoly on violence or compulsion has traditionally been how both domestic and foreign decisions as well as the decisions of private dispute resolution processes such as arbitration awards are concluded.

National decisions gain enforceability after they are given by the courts according to national legislation. The element of enforceability is embedded in the legal due process and so can rely upon the decision's finality and authority, the so-called *res judicata* effect. To clarify, *res judicata* is a legal concept used both in common law and civil law jurisdictions. It refers to the finality of a non-appealable judgment, precluding the possibility of further litigation in the same issue between the same parties. When a final decision has been rendered and all means of appeal have been exhausted or the appeal deadlines have expired, the decision is both enforceable and has *res judicata* effect.

Arbitration awards usually enter the state system by a different summary process known as *exequatur* established by the 1958 New York Convention. The Convention establishes the conditions that need to be met before the contracting states may recognize and enforce the award. The award is often declared enforceable in a summary process at a state court of jurisdiction. National legislation defines the right authority and protocol for this procedure. Thus, applying the New York Convention requires co-operation between the cross-border instrument and national legislation. At the time of writing, the convention has 156 parties.

There are other instruments for the recognition and enforcement of foreign decisions, such as the EU's Brussels Regulation (1215/2012) for the EU Member States. The recast Brussels I Regulation applies to recognizing and enforcing foreign judgments on civil and commercial matters within the EU Member States without resorting to a separate exequatur process. The objective is to further facilitate what is known as the free movement of decisions within the European legal area whereby a decision made in one country applies in another without the need for further legal argument and expense.

The advantage of state enforcement mechanisms is that they safeguard due process and only grant access to enforcement to decisions that are reached through fair and established practice. However, such instruments do not clearly establish a process for enforcing decisions of private ODR schemes.

Three Reasons Why Not

There are three reasons behind this. Firstly, ODR is such a new phenomenon that we do not have sufficient legal instruments such as multilateral conventions in place as of yet, as the drafting and signing of these instruments is a time-consuming and complicated matter. Secondly, there is a vast variety of different ODR procedures and platforms and a comprehensive over-arching business practice has yet to be created. Indeed, it is unclear whether formulating such a practice would be possible or even feasible, as there is so much variation between different schemes. Thirdly, enforcement through the state system relies upon the means to do so being both available and effective. This means that decisions can be put into practice by relatively simple measures such as distraining assets from a debtor's bank account. In comparison, out of court settlements may contain elements that cannot be enforced, e.g. apology. This is a similar issue as with alternative dispute resolution, where arbitration awards aim to be enforceable by the state enforcement mechanisms but in mediation the focus is on finding a satisfactory solution to all parties instead of deciding the legal facts and consequences.

Furthermore, state enforcement is not necessarily the only, or even the best, option for ODR processes. Still, it automatically provides a specific due process standard, which needs to be borne in mind as a part of the process design of other applications. A related issue is that litigation in national courts and public enforcement could be facilitated by implementation of courtroom technology, e.g. e-filing or electronic case management systems. Such reforms could make public enforcement a more feasible option for typical ODR situations as well.

Interface between ODR and Enforcement

The interface between ODR and enforcement has not received much attention in legal literature. It has been suggested that ODR decisions could be interpreted as arbitral awards and then enforced through the NY Convention mechanism we referenced above. However, the Convention imposes strict requirements for arbitration clauses and conduct of arbitration proceedings, and it is still unclear whether the scope of the Convention could be expanded to ODR. This discussion, whether ODR decisions could be enforced as arbitration awards, has been going on in UNCITRAL's working group III, which has negotiated unified procedural rules for ODR since 2010.

Alternative Ways to Gain Compliance

The relatively slow pace of state enforcement and the inefficiency and expense of cross-border enforcement has led to a situation where alternative ways of forcing compliance have emerged. Such alternatives do not necessarily lead to efficient outcomes in individual cases, but they aim to improve the operation of e-commerce and to increase trust between sellers and buyers. These alternatives include chargeback systems, user reviews, private enforcement and other means aimed to increase voluntary compliance or intervention, which I will discuss shortly. As the dispute resolution market and the interface between law and technology develop, other technology-enabled alternatives will most likely emerge. Regardless, there is still a tendency to see enforcement through the state-governed model.

It should be noted that these new alternatives are not considered enforcement in the traditional sense of the word, which are still taken as referring to the state's enforcement mechanisms. Instead they focus on providing easy to use and efficient conflict management to the online market right through to final resolution. Still, they at least partly serve the same objectives as the possibility of public enforcement – they aim to improve the quality of goods and services and improve predictability in case of transaction problems, and encourage trust within the markets or schemes where they are used. Increasing consumer trust in cross-border markets is also the objective behind EU's ADR Directive and ODR Regulation. According to the preamble of the ADR Directive

(2013/11/EU), improved trust would be essential for the development of the internal market.

Voluntary Compliance and User Reviews

The alternative dispute resolution movement of the 1980s highlighted the importance of finding a satisfactory resolution over the win-lose decision usually reached through the courts. The logic behind this was that more innovative outcomes more often lead to voluntary compliance with that outcome and thus avoid official enforcement completely. ODR has added a new layer to the scope of voluntary compliance through the introduction of user review systems. Based on public user experience comments and ratings, an e-commerce auction site promotes transparency and trust between buyers and sellers, encouraging compliance with the threat of bad reviews. The rationale is that best rated sellers get most future transactions, which in turn forces sellers to up their game. Examples of how this works are given in Katherine Newcomers' chapter "Online Dispute Resolution Decision Making – A NetNeutrals Practitioner's View."

User review systems are a good supplementary solution to promote trust on an e-commerce site, but they do not provide the complete answer for individual cases where, say, financial redress is demanded. Also, the question of unjust reviews is important: the possibilities of fraud, buying good reviews, threatening with bad reviews and other kinds of bad faith uses of the system are possible. In addition to the actual review system, a redress mechanism for managing fraudulent reviews is often needed. So we can see that a user review system alone cannot provide the complete solution.

Chargebacks

Chargebacks refer to the returning funds to a consumer, initiated by the credit card company in case a transaction done with the card has gone awry. Chargeback mechanisms are mostly used in the USA and the UK, The advantages of connecting dispute resolution with the payment mechanism are its easy accessibility and consumer awareness of its existence, the ease of binding the sellers to use the dispute resolution system, and the possibility of charging higher fees from the sellers who have repeated chargebacks and thus funding the mechanism without consumer fees.

It is unclear whether chargeback mechanisms could be adopted throughout European context, due to remaining differences in regulatory and economic frameworks. However, it is apparent that designing a chargeback mechanism as an enforcement alternative requires co-operation between different market operators probably within a statutory framework.

Private Enforcement and Technological Infrastructure

Some alternatives to public enforcement have already established their role in ODR. The most interesting example of these is private enforcement, a relatively new phenomenon that provides an interesting example of combining technological infrastructure with the dispute resolution process.

The online auction site eBay's Resolution Center, later on renamed "Money Back Guarantee", is an often-quoted example of successful ODR. This success is difficult to contradict, as eBay resolves over 60.000.000 e-commerce disputes annually. The system refunds a dissatisfied buyer in case the seller and buyer can't reach a solution themselves. In the end, the seller is then responsible for reimbursing the amount to eBay. Based on eBay's User Agreement of 12.8.2014, eBay may then request the interfaced payment operator PayPal to hold the seller's funds to enforce the seller's responsibility.

This connection between payment management and the e-commerce giant's dispute resolution system enables the formation of a private enforcement mechanism that does not require interaction with public courts. This means that the infrastructure necessitated by eBay's combination of a payment mechanism, dispute resolution system and auction site requires a large-scale operation.

The idea behind private enforcement is innovative: technology is harnessed to provide automated enforcement after the ODR process has reached an outcome. However, this idea could go further, with the emerging possibility of combining an automated technological infrastructure for dispute resolution with an interface to a payment mechanism.

The Bitcoin Example

Ways of managing this interface in the future could be facilitated with new and creative software development: for example, trust could be allocated *by* the infrastructure *to* the infrastructure, instead of simply improving trust between the sellers and buyers through a mutual review process. This could be achieved in the same way as the decentralized digital currency *Bitcoin*, where the currency itself includes both a cryptographically secure ledger or *block chain* of all earlier transactions, and the possibility of creating e.g. decentralized digital contracts and escrow services. Whereas the authority and trust in traditional currency is ascertained by the credibility of central banks, digital currency achieves this by authenticating the ownership by the protocol itself. François R. Velde writes in his article 'Bitcoin: A Primer', "Bitcoin solves two challenges of digital money – controlling its creation and avoiding its duplication – at once" Before a transaction is added to the block chain, it has to include a solution to a mathematical problem, which is difficult to solve but the solution is easy to verify. As validation of the currency is difficult and costly, individuals doing it are rewarded by new bitcoins. Thus, there is no central registry of earlier transactions nor does the reliability of the currency depend on a centralized authority. The same logic of decentralized verifiability and code-induced conflict prevention has been applied to smart contracts and escrows by Ethereum, which describes itself as *"a decentralized platform that runs smart contracts: applications that run exactly as programmed without any possibility of downtime, censorship, fraud or third party interference."*

The logical next step is to examine, whether lessons learned from the Bitcoin example could be applied to dispute resolution and enforcement. This could mean that the credibility and fairness of ODR decisions could be verified by the technological infrastructure itself without resorting to any external agency or to court assessment in processes. Such applications could provide less fallible indicators of fairness than user review systems, chargebacks or public enforcement. The ODR process itself would verify its fairness and enforceability – and lead directly to automated enforcement. Still, in order to translate ideas into practice, such possibilities regarding dispute resolution and enforcement should be explored both from a regulatory and a software development perspective.

The Connection between Enforcement and System Design

The previous examples illustrate that there are more possibilities of forcing compliance than simply going through public enforcement mechanisms. However, the advantages of national enforcement systems, especially the respect of due process, should not be overlooked. In any case, the fairness of both the actual dispute resolution system and the enforcement mechanism has to be taken into consideration.

The needs of the actual users and their experience of the fairness of the system are a significant part of the system's credibility. As is especially apparent in cross-border cases, going to court is often not a feasible option, and there is the risk that an ODR solution, regardless of its binding or unbinding nature, is the only actual possibility of finding redress for e-commerce cases. This further accentuates the importance of fairness in ODR procedures.

It follows from due process standards, that in most jurisdictions use of force (or legal compulsion) is closely regulated. In addition to these regulatory frameworks, the questions of privacy and data protection form the regulatory framework for ODR and enforcement. It is essential to see the resolution of an individual case as a unified process bringing together both dispute resolution and enforcement, to ensure compliance with the outcome mandated in the decision.

A key element of designing such an extensive system of dispute resolution and enforcement is to understand the variety of different alternative enforcement mechanisms and their strengths and weaknesses. Also, different mechanisms require action at different stages of the dispute's timeline, which directly affects both process design and software development. For example, enforcement through the state's mechanism is relatively straightforward but requires compatibility with the official court system and awareness of its practices. In comparison, private enforcement mechanisms require more detailed design, as forced compliance is not "outsourced" to the state mechanism. In any case, decisions regarding enforcement interfaces must take place before detailed process design.

Conclusions

Bringing technology into dispute resolution has altered our way of understanding both dispute resolution and enforcement. The increase of cross-border transactions and the use of technology have brought increasing amounts of low intensity disputes in their wake. Allocating trust and improving compliance with codes of conduct in general is an essential part of designing online environments. This dispute resolution environment has created a need for new ways of designing conflict management as a whole. This new process design, which aims at developing software that can facilitate or completely manage disputes, differs significantly from the traditional legal processes of trials and courts.

The changing environment of dispute resolution also enables different methods for forcing compliance than resorting to the state enforcement mechanism. Private enforcement is a new item on the agenda and it is still unclear exactly how it will or even can be regulated. Chargebacks are an US model that is still mostly unknown in Europe, and their application depends on the interaction of several players in the relevant markets and an analysis of the whole European situation and best practices. User reviews are a relatively simple way of increasing transparency but come with several weaknesses: they do not provide an efficient solution for enforcement in a single case, and the risk of misuse of the review system has to be addressed.

Ultimately, this all translates into the need to see enforcement as an integral part of the dispute resolution process, and to understand enforcement's role in creating trust amongst users. As such, enforcement and other alternatives of providing trust in online transactions need to be thought of as a part of the design of the whole system.

The Experience of Combining Traditional Face to Face Dispute Resolution Mediation with an Online Dispute Resolution Tool – Benefits and Challenges

Amy H. Koltz, J.D

Executive Director and Mediator for Metro Milwaukee Mediation Services, Inc.

Case Study: Homeowner under threat from poor mortgage renegotiation process

Homeowner A was a single parent, self-employed as a consultant and a part-time maths teacher. She spent 263 days actively engaged in mediation from mid-2012 to mid-2013. At each new session, the representative of the mortgage company was a different individual. The representative would indicate one of the following 1) the documentation was complete and underwriting needed more time to conduct the review, 2) the documentation was incomplete based on a never before requested item, or 3) the documentation was incomplete because previously provided documents were now outdated. Homeowner A would provide the requested items within 24 hours, sometimes even during the mediation session. However, during each new session, it appeared Homeowner A's file hadn't been touched since the prior session. This was the case in spite of the fact we would adjourn the mediation sessions out 30-45 days for the servicer to review the file and render a decision.

Homeowner A did ultimately receive a loan modification. But, if it took this long for a diligent homeowner, with the assistance of a trained attorney-mediator, to get a loan modification with this servicer, how could the average homeowner navigate the system alone? Further, the 6-month redemption period had expired, so the servicer could have held the sheriff's sale to repossess the property within three weeks, had there been no agreement. Consequently, Homeowner A would have had little time to plan or prepare for that result. There had to be a better way.

The U.S. Mortgage Foreclosure Crisis

Parties in Chaos

The United States mortgage foreclosure crisis began in 2007.[1] The average U.S. citizen facing mortgage foreclosure did not know where to turn for help, other than to the organisations holding their mortgages (we will call them mortgage servicers), whose infrastructures were not able to cope with the high volume of mortgagees needing assistance. The result, parties in chaos.

The parties' inability to communicate reliably and effectively hindered efforts to resolve foreclosures or mitigate other potential loss.

The Initial Response

In response, foreclosure mediation programmes were introduced in some parts of the USA. These were designed to shepherd homeowners through the mortgage servicer's loan modification review process and facilitate discussion of home retention options, or to facilitate a graceful exit from the property, leaving the homeowner with some sense of dignity and respect. The Milwaukee Foreclosure Mediation Program was launched in 2009. The result of this stakeholder-designed, court-based programme was a process with a high-level of buy-in and participation by servicers and their local legal counsel, despite the voluntary nature of the initiative.

However, the process was plagued by complications around the paperwork needed at the mediation sessions in order for the mortgage servicer to assess mortgage modification options. Consequently, there were often repeated adjournments so that documentation could be supplied in the form needed. There always appeared to be something missing resulting in sometimes upwards of seven or more sessions, spanning months, occasionally over a year. This increased the risk of forced repossession and sale. Something had to change.

The Next Step - Combining Traditional Dispute Resolution and Online Dispute Resolution

It was clear we needed a tool to streamline the document collection and exchange, so mediation could be as efficient as intended. Although set up as a traditional, face-to-face mediation process, we subsequently implemented a hybrid process, combining traditional dispute resolution and online dispute resolution. This was done with an eye towards gaining efficiencies and better overall resolutions.

DMM Loss Mitigation Web Portal (Portal), is an online product of Default Mitigation Management, LLC. The product was originally developed for use in bankruptcy proceedings and in particular for mortgage modifications mediations as part of that process. Advantages of the Portal include 1) the ability for streamlined communications with all parties connected securely through the Portal, direct submission of labelled and dated documentation, and real-time communications, 2) transparency with all stakeholders seeing the same information and an objective record of all transactions, and 3) cost savings through increased efficiencies, faster resolutions, lower document transmission costs (than mailing overnight packages) and lower FTE (full time equivalent) staff costs. Further, the technological advantage of the Portal is that it is web-based and does not require any special equipment or software to install. The Portal also offers added features that enhance the financial package preparation process, called docUmods™, described as Turbo Tax for financial packages, and the DMM DOCU*MENTOR*™, which enables splitting and uniformly labelling financial package components with ease.

The mediation programme engages numerous stakeholders with varied interests. Mediation programme upper management determined that the Portal would enhance and streamline the mediation process enabling us to help the parties overcome the primary factor causing delay in the loan modification review process – incomplete or seemingly incomplete financial documentation packages. Next came the work of fostering buy-in with key stakeholders and implementing Portal usage as a required part of the mediation process with some new rules.

Document Disciplines and Timelines

These new rules provided that upon the mortgage servicer's consent to participate in the programme on a given case, the homeowner's financial package was uploaded into the Portal, where documents were labelled in a uniform fashion and saved with identifying names and corresponding upload dates. The rules also set timelines by which the servicer needed to notify through the Portal any requests for additional documentation, and by which the homeowner needed to provide that documentation. Rather than being presented with a large, unlabelled PDF document the parties now had access to individual, labelled documents in a secure, password-protected forum. Further, the Portal allowed the mediator, mediation administration, counsel for the parties, the housing counsellor, and the servicer representative to communicate in real-time with messages that would generate emails to the case participants, and also capture the message contents and history on the case page itself.

Since the Portal implementation was undertaken as part of a state-wide programme expansion, additional stakeholders included civil circuit court judges throughout the state and the Wisconsin Department of Justice Consumer Protection Division and Office of the Attorney General. Their support was a critical element in requiring use of the Portal amongst mortgage servicers. The local servicers' attorneys' participation in this roll-out was similarly critical for the influence they could exert over their clients to participate in our voluntary programme and use the Portal as required. The Mediation Programme's strong track record for fairness and neutrality, along with the rapport the Executive Director Debra Tuttle developed and maintained with key DOJ and local foreclosure law firm personnel, went a long way toward fostering the transition. Another aspect of the transition involved demonstrating the Portal to housing counsellors, mediation administration staff and mediators and discussing how each of these groups would ultimately incorporate using the Portal.

With the ability to provide the financials in a uniform, organized fashion and to receive real-time updates from the servicer representative, it was now possible for the servicer to render a loan modification decision on the file even prior to the mediation session. In those instances, the initial mediation session involved discussion of an offer, rather than a discussion of the documentation needed. This was the type of streamlined process foreclosure mediation was intended to offer. However, the Portal was not fully embraced by all stakeholders in the fashion we envisioned.

Resistance

Housing counsellors were an integral part of our process, meeting face-to-face with homeowners and assisting them with compiling the necessary financials and forms to initiate the loan modification process through mediation, and providing the counselling and advocacy advice that the mediation programme staff, as neutrals, could not. They were using different systems and did not take advantage of the DMM Portal to create client records and upload financial information directly to the Portal. Their primary concern was document duplication and loss of efficiency. Although housing counsellor use of the Portal did not turn out as we anticipated, this was a minor setback that ultimately did not diminish the value of the Portal to the foreclosure mediation programme participants.

Varying Degrees of Acceptance

On the whole, servicers participating in our programme do use the Portal. This can be attributed to the benefits of the Portal to servicers and their local counsel. The adoption of the Portal by local legal offices is a reflection of their confidence in the benefits of our foreclosure mediation process in general. Finally, participation in our programme requires use of the Portal, and this requirement is endorsed by the local courts. However, participating servicers do so to varying degrees. Particularly early on, the servicers would simply have their local counsel use the portal to retrieve and download files to then fax to the servicer or upload into the Black Knight system, which is widely used for communication and documents exchange between servicers and their attorneys. Some servicers continue to take this approach. Other servicers will retrieve the documentation from the portal; but not communicate through it. Instead, documents requests go through the mail and/or by phone to the homeowner. Documents requests also often come through local counsel's office to our office, for communication to the homeowner. This defeats some of the efficiency that can be gained through proper use of the Portal. Another challenge we've seen is that individuals within the servicing corporation who have access to the Portal are not the individuals in the mediation department who communicate what's missing or what's needed during the mediation session.

Some resistance to the intended method of using the Portal could be attributed to concerns regarding security, confidentiality and transparency. Security is an easy first objection, particularly when private financial records are involved. Further, when parties are already in the process of litigation, there are certainly concerns regarding how shared information will be used and if it could end up as evidence in court.

Anticipating and Overcoming Implementation Challenges and Recommendations

On the whole, we accomplished our goals of integrating the Portal to gain efficiencies in the mediation process. However, it was at times a delicate balancing act when working with so many disparate stakeholders, particularly in the context of a voluntary mediation process. We needed to minimize the potential for stakeholders to walk away from the programme. The process of anticipating and addressing potential reasons for resistance, managing expectations, and making adjustments based on stakeholder input was essential to this initiative.

Factors to Consider When Assessing ODR Tools or Systems

Based on our experience, here are some examples of factors to consider when assessing ODR tools or systems and anticipating potential causes of resistance.

- ACCESS –

    o who has access,

    o how do users gain access,

    o who manages access,

    o are special computer system capabilities necessary,

    o can the system accommodate all parties to the dispute

- SECURITY –

    o is the content secure and confidential,

    o what mechanisms are in place to ensure confidentiality and security,

    o what does authentication entail – 1-step or 2-step log-in process,

    o will security measures impede ease of access for intended users

- INTEGRATION –

    o will system work with existing equipment/programmes?

    o will system create redundancy in workflow?

- ○ will system displace existing systems?

- ○ will system require additional or fewer staff?

- ○ will system require extensive training?

- • EXPOSURE –

  - ○ will the system create potential liability or exposure for disputing parties?

Reflections

Looking back at how the Mediation Programme worked with the various stakeholders to incorporate Portal usage into the existing Foreclosure Mediation process, it becomes clear that adding new technology into an existing programme, process, or framework is not as simple as designating a product and then using it. Riiki Koulu makes the point in her chapter that "designing a dispute resolution system is a delicate interplay between several interest groups". The fashion in which the new technology is designed or selected, introduced, and implemented is critical to how fully those using the technology embrace it, if at all. Resisting change seems a natural part of human behaviour and when it comes to incorporating new technology in the workplace, potential for resistance can be particularly high. We faced a particularly daunting challenge of implementing this tool for use by different government funded not for profit organisations, law firms, and mortgage servicers. But in the end the effort is still worth it.

3 Key Take-away Points:

1. An ODR system may perfectly match your needs, but don't assume everyone will share your enthusiasm,

2. It is natural for people to resist change, particularly those on the "front-lines", but don't be discouraged,

3. It is possible to convert resistance into commitment and enthusiasm with careful planning and this planning is important because you need **people** to make the technology work.

Chapter Notes

[i] A general synopsis of the subprime mortgage crisis from 2007 to 2010, can be found on the Federal Reserve History website, available at http://www.federalreservehistory.org/Events/DetailView/55.

Online Dispute Resolution Decision Making – A NetNeutrals Practitioner's View

Katherine G. Newcomer

Member of the New Jersey Bar, her practice specialises in conflict mediation and arbitration

Introduction: the Rules of the Game

Online Dispute Resolution (ODR) is available for eBay members through a program called NetNeutrals. NetNeutrals has specific limitations and criteria. Available only to Sellers, the facility makes decisions about the fairness or accuracy of feedback about items that cost over one thousand dollars to buy. NetNeutrals charges a $130 fee for this review process. Both the Claimant (the Seller) and the Respondent (the Buyer) can present their side on an Independent Feedback Review (IFR) forum and can also include attached documents relevant to their case. In addition, the Arbitrator (known as 'the Neutral' in NetNeutral parlance) can see the eBay Member to Member messages (M2Ms) as part of the review process. However, the Arbitrator does not engage with the parties – no questions are put to them directly. The Arbitrator relies on their position statements in making a decision.

This chapter will explore the decision making process in regard to the four criteria established by eBay for decisions both about feedback removal and we will also look at the circumstances when the feedback stands and is not to be removed.

The impact of feedback in the eBay context is considerable. For the Seller, feedback determines whether or not a Buyer will even choose to purchase from them. Few people will purchase from a Seller with a negative rating. For the Buyer, it is their opportunity to be heard and express their view about the Seller and the transaction. Both of these aspects of feedback can have deep meaning to the parties. Often members can become very emotional and their position statements can become abusive and insulting.

Criterion One:

The Member leaving the feedback did not demonstrate a good faith effort to complete the transaction

For the purposes of the IFR forum, a "good faith effort" to complete the transaction involves three things:

1) Paying the deposit on time;

2) Paying the remaining balance as per the Seller's policy; and

3) Taking possession of the vehicle or item that was purchased for over $1000.

The reasoned basis for removing feedback under the criterion of not making a good faith effort to complete the transaction is as follows:

1) A reasonable person who reads negative feedback related for example to a purchase of a vehicle will presume that the Buyer who has made this complaint is now in possession of the vehicle and therefore is fully up to speed with the details of the vehicle's condition.

2) If the Buyer never took possession of the vehicle, the credibility of any negative feedback related to the vehicle's condition would be undermined, and a future customer's reasonable presumption regarding the Buyer's possession of the vehicle would be false.

Usually, this criterion is cut and dried. If the Buyer did not follow through with the purchase, the feedback will not stand.

Case One:

A Buyer left the following feedback: "never returned my phone calls open claim ebay helped me out thanks." However, according to the M2M messages, the Buyer chose not to move forward with the transaction. He informed the Seller that he needed to cancel his purchase as his two children were ill in hospital and that his medical bills were piling up. The Seller provided attachments that included an eBay cancelled sale notice, a screenshot of his call to the Buyer, a copy of the M2Ms, amongst other relevant documents. Additionally, the Arbitrator can look at the eBay listing and review the Seller's stated policy. In this case, the Seller offered a refund if the Buyer was not satisfied with the vehicle. This Seller gave his Buyer a full refund. The Buyer chose not to explain his position in the forum. This decision was quite simple and the criteria for feedback removal were met and the feedback was withdrawn.

Case Two:

The Buyer stated in his feedback that the Seller was dishonest. He had driven 460 miles to get this bike, and it was not as described. The charge of dishonesty or fraud is serious and requires a high bar to stand. Criterion One applied as the Buyer decided not take possession of the motorcycle. Upon inspection, he found that the listing description did not match the condition of the vehicle. Even though the Seller immediately refunded his deposit, the buyer was unhappy with having driven so far. While an Arbitrator should consider a Buyer's disappointment about driving a distance and finding that the $14,000 motorcycle he was keen to buy was not to his satisfaction, the criterion for removal was met on three counts: he had a complete refund; did not pay for nor take possession of the motorcycle.

Case Three:

The Buyer stated in his feedback that "Vehicle not inspected as required by state law. Reported to NC Dept of Justice." In this case, both parties participated in the forum. Judging by their position statements, the transaction was difficult on both sides. According to the Buyer, he had been concerned that the 1996 Jaguar had not been inspected before being offered for sale, as required by North Carolina law. The Seller disclosed in the vehicle listing that it had not been inspected. Once the Seller realized that the vehicle had been improperly offered for sale, he withdrew the transaction and refunded the Buyer's deposit after a week and half. The Buyer remained interested in the vehicle. The Seller invested about half the value of the vehicle ($1,500) effecting repairs so that it could pass inspection. It took three weeks for the work to be completed and the vehicle was offered to the Buyer again. The Buyer lost confidence in the Seller when he did not personally attend the Buyer's inspection of the vehicle at the dealership. At this point, the Buyer chose not to proceed with the sale. As a result, this case clearly fell under into Criterion One – despite the inspection issues that were reported to the North Carolina Department of Justice. Even though the legal issues cloud the case, the facts of the matter fit Criterion One. However, it seemed prudent to make note of the problems with the inspection by stating that the IFR forum only deals with feedback. The substantive issue of offering a vehicle for sale in North Carolina that had not been inspected is beyond scope of the forum. The decision was framed narrowly to focus only on the issue regarding feedback and how it met the requirements of Criterion One.

Case Four:

This is a case that could have been decided through Criterion One or Two. As an example, this account is presented in the decision format used by NetNeutrals. Context for the feedback is provided by the type of vehicle or item over $1000, the selling price, the mileage (or condition of the item), and the date of the sale. The identities of the Buyer and Seller are not given and identifying details of the case removed.

Case File Decision Format Example

> *Based on a review the information presented, it is the opinion of this Neutral that the feedback DOES meet the criteria for feedback removal. The vehicle in this transaction is a 2013 Ford XXXXX with 19,177 miles. It sold at auction on January XX, 2014 for $14,980.00 with a Manufacturer's Warranty. In the feedback, the Buyer, XXXXXX, states that he or she tried to cancel bid, by email, by phone. The Seller, XXXXXX, disputes this feedback. There is clear and convincing evidence in the forum, the vehicle listing, and the M2M messages that suggests that the member leaving the feedback did not demonstrate a good faith effort to complete the transaction. Both parties participated in the forum. In the M2M messages, the Buyer asked for the Seller to cancel his or her bid as their financing fell through. In the second M2M message, the Buyer asks for the Seller to cancel the transaction due to a medical emergency which required a leave of absence on his or her part. In addition, in the forum, the Buyer states that he or she will remove the feedback since the Seller did cancel the transaction. The logical basis for removing feedback under the criterion of not making a good faith effort to complete the transaction is as follows: 1.) A reasonable person who reads negative feedback related to a vehicle will presume that the Buyer who has made this complaint is now in possession of the vehicle and therefore knows the intimate details of the vehicle's condition. 2.) If the Buyer never took possession of the vehicle, the credibility of any negative feedback related to the vehicle's condition would be undermined, and a future customer's reasonable presumption regarding the Buyer's possession of the vehicle would be false. Therefore, the criteria for feedback removal have been met and the feedback shall be withdrawn.*

While the fact pattern clearly fell under Criterion One, it also could have been decided under Criterion Two.

Criterion Two:

The feedback was not submitted in a reasonable amount of time.

Previously, thirty days was considered ample to time to leave feedback. However, eBay has instructed NetNeutrals that feedback may be added up to sixty days after the auction end. This is especially useful when there have been difficulties with the transaction resulting in emails over time, repair issues, title delays, etc. Normally, eBay will not allow feedback to be left over sixty days through its software platform. NetNeutrals has seen cases where feedback left prematurely, prevented or discouraged the Seller from addressing the complaint that forms the basis of the negative feedback. In Case Four, the Buyer states that he or she will remove the negative feedback because the Seller satisfied her request to cancel the transaction. Such a statement by a Buyer also will satisfy the requirements of Criterion Two. In this case, the Arbitrator had a choice of criteria. Criterion One appeared to present the strongest rationale so it was employed. In many cases, more than one criterion will fit the fact pattern. The most definitive and logical criterion should be utilized.

Criterion Three:

There is evidence to suggest that the transaction-related information contained in the feedback column is factually inaccurate.

This criterion can be the most difficult to determine. The question of who is telling the truth arises in many cases. Often, the nature of the feedback will determine whether or not it will stand.

Case Five:

The Buyer wrote his feedback in capital letters and stated: "BIGGEST LIARS. WON'T CALL BACK, THIS WILL COST ME THOUSANDS. STAY CLEAR OF THEM." This case involved a motorhome that sold as a "Buy It Now" price of $79,000 and low mileage.

Both parties participated in the forum. The Seller stated in the forum that the motorhome was sold with a third party warranty and "as is." It was inspected by a third party, but was brought back to the dealership and repaired at no cost to the Buyer. Additionally, the Seller notes that the third party warranty would cover any additional repairs. The Buyer did not submit any work orders or estimates to the Seller or forum. It appeared that the Seller had tried to satisfy the Buyer. Additionally, the Seller has submitted evidence of a $250.00 refund where upon acceptance of the refund, the Buyer agrees to have the feedback removed. However, it appeared that the Buyer did not do so. The Seller states in the forum that they at no time lied or failed to call him back and argued that the feedback was defamatory in nature. While the Buyer did participate in the forum, he appeared to be waiting for a question to be asked of him rather than presenting his side of the transaction. The Seller's position appeared more credible. Electrical repairs had been made free of charge, a third party warranty was in place, a concession had been offered and accepted, and use of the term "Biggest Liars" appeared not to be justified. Included in the decision was the statement: "… the expression "Biggest Liars" is a serious one and appears to cross the line. Such language can be construed as insulting and is not helpful to the eBay community."

Because of the derogatory language, a higher standard of evidence would be required to justify it. The Seller's position statement and written proof of concession was more persuasive.

Case Six:

Sometimes only one aspect of the feedback is inaccurate. The feedback in this case involved a car with high mileage. The Buyer wrote: "vehicle not as described, seller did not have title; vehicle in horrible condition." Only the Seller participated in the forum. According to the M2M messages, the Seller had fully disclosed that he would not have the title available when the Buyer arrived to pick up the vehicle on a Sunday. The Buyer both understood and agreed to these terms. Since the feedback was inaccurate in regards to the title issue, Criterion Three applied and the feedback did not stand. The issue about the condition and description of the vehicle did not enter into the decision.

Case Seven:

Often cases under this criterion are not clear cut. In this case, the Buyer states that the vehicle is not as described, many interior and outside scratches that were not disclosed, and has a dog smell.

The vehicle in this transaction was an older car with relatively high mileage and was sold "as is" and no warranty. Because the Buyer both personally inspected the car for three hours and paid for an independent inspection, it would appear that the Buyer should have been aware of any defects and could have addressed them properly at the time of purchase. The Seller states in the forum that the Buyer contacted him three weeks after taking possession about the dog smell and requested $500.00 to remedy the problem. The Seller agreed to send out some odour eliminator, but the Buyer left negative feedback before he could do so. The Buyer contends that he alerted the Seller the next day about the dog odour. The M2M messages, the photos, and the forum were reviewed carefully. For a vehicle with over six model years and over 100,000 miles, it appeared to be mechanically sound with an exterior and an interior in good shape. The Seller did disclose that there was some wear due to mileage and year. Coupled with the fact that the vehicle was both inspected by the Buyer and an independent mechanic, it would appear that the Buyer was satisfied with the vehicle's condition at purchase. His concerns seem to have come afterwards. However, this case could have also been decided under Criterion Four – as the demand for $500.00 to get rid of dog odour seemed an attempt to extract excessive value.

Criterion Four:

The member leaving the feedback made an attempt to extract excessive value from the other party.

This criterion can also be difficult to determine as Sellers often attempt to garner positive feedback with concessions or offers and the Buyers will try to have the condition of the vehicle or item improved. While it is the Seller's prerogative to obtain as many positive feedbacks as possible, the Buyers may counter these solicitations by holding out for some level of compensation. Generally, these exchanges are readily accessible in the M2M messages. Sometimes the Buyers' attempts to obtain value become more akin to "extortion" where the Buyers' demands – often accompanied by a suggestion of further exposure through other social media channels -suggest an attempt to gain "excessive value".

The most frequent examples of excessive value are:

1) Demanding travel costs;

2) Repair costs for maintenance that are common with older vehicles; and

3) Requesting money for repairs after having already received money from the Seller.

It is not extortion for Buyers to request that Sellers reimburse them for repairs that were made to bring the vehicle up to the standards of the listing details. The exception is for maintenance issues that would include tires, brakes, fluids, etc. Mechanical repairs would include engine, transmission, suspension, etc. However, the Buyers should present the Sellers with either a work order or repair estimate from a properly licensed mechanic, rather than pull a number from the air.

Case Eight:

In this case, the Buyer left feedback that states: "I was RIPPED OFF & seller refuses to do anything about the undisclosed dents." The vehicle in this transaction was a 2002 Thunderbird with low mileage. It was sold for $11,500 as a best offer accepted and with no warranty. The Buyer found numerous problems including air conditioning, dents, and check engine light being on. He asks for at least $4,000 to $4,500 to repair these undisclosed issues, yet he did not give the Seller any estimates or work orders. Because the Buyer asked for almost half the value of the vehicle without submitting any proof, the fact pattern seemed to fit well into Criterion Four. Unfortunately, the Buyer did not participate in the forum.

Case Nine:

The Buyer states in the feedback: "BEWARE! Misleading AND dishonest communication -- car needs $5,000 in repairs." The vehicle in this case was a 1995 Mercedes that sold for $3,650.00 In the M2M messages, the Buyer states that he had already spent $800 replacing fuel lines, the battery, and repairing the driver side rear door window. He demands $1,500 to revise his negative feedback but does not present any work orders or repair estimates. The Seller offered $40.00 to replace the battery. In the M2M messages, the Buyer initially thought that that the twenty year old car actually needs $7,000 in repairs. This case appeared to fall under Criterion Four because the Buyer did not present the Seller with any work orders and his expectations were disproportionate as he asked for close to half of the selling price. The Buyer did not present his or her point of view in the forum.

Case Ten:

In this case, the Buyer is extremely passionate about his transaction. He demands $2,500 to remove his negative feedback. The Buyer is adamant about his negative experience and states that he will not stop even if the Seller accepts the vehicle back or fixes it partially so he can use the car. The Buyer states that he has left negative feedback everywhere that he can and has reported the Seller to the police. The Seller alerted the same police department as the Buyer also left him death threats. The negative feedback that was given asserts that the Buyer did not receive the title for two weeks, and that the phone was not answered, that he left tons of messages, and that $21,000 car runs as a tractor. The Buyer insists that the Seller should 'eat any' costs incurred and restore the vehicle to its brand new condition. This fact pattern could have fit either Criterion Three or Four as the title issue was explained by Buyer's changing his mind about which address needed to be on the document. As a result, the title's delivery was delayed as it needed to be changed. However, the case was decided under Criterion Four due to Buyer's excessive expectations. Normally, when faced with a choice between those two criteria, Criterion Three is less inflammatory to the parties than Four. One could imagine that few would wish to be labelled as a person who attempts to extract excessive value from another party.

Where the Finding is: Feedback Stands

When the feedback is not to be removed, all four criteria are considered in making the final determination. It is important to review each of the criterion so as to be clear that all aspects of the Seller's position have been considered carefully. As the protocol for denying feedback removal is more involved, an example is helpful, drawing on the case documents.

Case Eleven:

Based on a review of the information presented, it is the opinion of this Neutral that the feedback DOES NOT meet the criteria for feedback removal. This transaction involves a vintage 1959 Chevrolet Corvette four speed. It sold on eBay on June XX, 2014 for $48,000.00 with mileage of 33,369. It was sold without an existing warranty. Both parties participated in the forum. The forum, the vehicle listing, and the M2Ms contain a lack of clear and convincing evidence that would suggest that the guidelines for feedback removal have been met. The Buyer, XXXXX, states in his or her negative feedback on August XX, 2014 that "Simply desapointed, MOTOR defect, not mentioned on the add." The Seller, XXXXX, disputes this feedback. 1.) A good faith effort appears to have been made to complete the transaction. From the feedback, the Buyer appears to have taken possession of the vehicle. The Buyer received the vehicle eighteen days after auction end. 2.) The feedback was left in a timely manner. According to eBay policy, thirty (30) days is usually an adequate time to allow Buyers to inspect vehicles, take possession of the vehicle, and to leave feedback. Some flexibility is allowed for feedback to be given – generally up to sixty days for certain reasonable circumstances. This feedback was given on the fiftieth day after the sale of the vehicle. However, given that the Buyer did not receive the car until eighteen days after it was sold, the Buyer gave the feedback after 32 days taking possession of the vehicle. In effect, the feedback was given on the 32nd day after taking possession of the vehicle and is within eBay's window of opportunity for feedback. 3.) There is a lack of evidence to suggest that the information contained in the feedback is inaccurate. The Buyer states that he is disappointed. The vehicle smokes and burns oil when it runs. The Buyer has determined that it needs new rings. The Buyer does not use inflammatory language. The vehicle was listed as being mechanically sound. The Seller was concerned that the Buyer might have damaged the engine while it was in his possession. The Buyer states that it was only driven three miles since it arrived from the shipping company. The Buyer submitted a photo where one can see smoke coming from the exhaust. 4.) There is a lack of evidence to suggest an extraction of excessive value. Even though the vehicle appears not to have met the listing standards, there is no evidence to suggest any such attempt. Based on the Forum, the vehicle listing, and the

M2M messages, this Neutral does not have enough evidence to remove the feedback. Based on all of this information, the feedback DOES NOT meet the criteria for feedback removal and shall not be withdrawn.

The nature of this feedback is matter of fact and not inflammatory. The Buyer expresses his/her disappointment without resorting to insulting language. The criteria for removal were not met.

Case Twelve:

The feedback simply states that the "Vehicle had many, many more issues than stated in description. Very disappointed." The vehicle was a 2008 Cadillac and was sold for $17,600 with what is called 'a rebuilt title'. A rebuilt title requires a heightened awareness on the part of a Buyer, suggesting as it does extensive damage to the vehicle in the past. After purchase, the Buyer discovered that the vehicle had been in a significant accident that required $22,000 worth of repairs. The Seller had advertised the vehicle as having a previous owner who had put water in the petrol tank. However, the Buyer also found evidence of flooding and submitted photographic proof of significant rusting. The Seller argued that the Buyer was not required to accept the vehicle as per the listing policy, but that does not obviate the Buyer's right to leave feedback based upon his or her experience. The tone of this feedback was restrained, kept to the facts, and is to the point. It did not fall under any other criteria and it stood.

Conclusion:

ODR involving feedback can be difficult because of the problems in ascertaining who is telling the truth. Often, there is not enough information, sometimes too much. Extraneous issues can be a distraction. The Arbitrator needs to keep the focus on the requirements of the criteria and not follow the Buyer down the rabbit hole of threats of legal action. That said, impartiality and fairness to both parties is paramount. Passions can flame high on the Internet. The safety of relative anonymity of the Buyers can encourage them to leave feedback that does not fit the criteria. NetNeutrals gives qualifying Sellers a last resort in protecting themselves and their business from unfair feedback. The ODR Arbitrator must find that balance between the Sellers' interests and the right of the Buyer to be heard. The Arbitrator is well advised to look first to the nature of the feedback and then determine if the fact pattern of the case falls under the requirements of the four criteria.

Points to Take Away

1. The Arbitrator must not be distracted by extraneous issues and keep the focus on the facts.

2. Part of the Arbitrator's job is to ascertain who is more likely to be telling the truth. Both parties might allow their belief in the rightness of their positions to tempt them into inaccuracy.

3. The Arbitrator should make every effort to employ tact, yet be firm. Often some language acknowledging the feelings of the Buyer can be useful.

4. Always, the Arbitrator must make every effort to be neutral and unbiased.

One Man's View of One Country – ADR & ODR and the future of complaint management in the UK

Adrian Lawes

Director - Consumerdata and Publisher/editor of Just about Travel

Gearing Up for the ADR Introduction in the UK

The Citizens Advice Bureau (CAB) is the main UK consumer advice service and is often the first port-of-call for anyone with a problem. According to their latest annual report and accounts they dealt with 1.2 million telephone enquiries; sixteen million people used their online services and two million people visited them in person. While not all of this traffic is concerned with complaints about goods and services, such queries are a significant part of the CAB's activities. The UK government – as part of the introduction of an alternative disputes resolution system – has recognised this and has provided more money to the CAB to enable training of its 21,500 volunteers and to raise awareness of the new systems for dispute resolution that come into play on October 1st 2015. My fellow authors have set out the details of the legal and institutional framework for this change and in particular the role of the EU and its Digital Single Market Strategy in fostering consumer confidence in cross-border trade within the EU.

In this chapter I will give a personal one-country overview of the UK complaint scene from the way complainant satisfaction is measured, complainant behaviour and the choices consumers with a problem have in terms of where to go to seek a remedy. Looking to the future of dispute resolution and the new procedures becoming available, I ask whether consumers will put their confidence in such schemes and on what grounds? Will their verdicts be wholly subjective perceptions of independence and competence or will they have access to more objective data? I anticipate innovation and competition arising from new entrants to the market challenging established means of obtaining redress such as the courts or the various established bodies in the UK handling complaints escalated to them. It has been quite some time since businesses and their customers in the UK considered the public courts as the default option for settling low value consumer issues even given the existence of a small claims procedure within the court system. What consequences – good or bad – can we expect from the introduction of new players into this arena?

The Online Opportunity

The size of the opportunity for online dispute resolution (ODR) in particular as a means of delivery of ADR within the UK, is undeniable. The data presented in the report OFCOM Communications Market 2015 show that 62% of UK adults had used the internet to make a purchase (32% in the last week). Rated by a measure based on visits to all the sites and apps owned by a particular concern, Amazon has an unique audience of 37million and eBay 31 – they are the fifth and seventh most popular by this measure. As reported in other chapters, a world wide provider of ODR, Modria, project there will be 1 billion online disputes by the year 2017. There are no data for cross-border transactions. But the high level of internet use for the purchase of goods and services is a fact within the UK is clear. Problems with online purchases need online solutions.

Depending on the item purchased or the service bought, according to research in the US and UK, that is detailed in the chapter by Marc Grainer, purchasers have had a variety of ways in which to complain. Retail outlets, cafes, restaurants, hotels, B&Bs, guesthouses and service stations have been the easiest to achieve a satisfactory outcome because the purchaser is on the spot and can argue about the problem there and then. Larger purchases and online bought products and services take longer to resolve but the improvement in customer service means that even some of these problems can be resolved with little delay.

Customer Satisfaction and Resolution

Are customers satisfied with the way complaints are handled now? The proliferation of customer satisfaction surveys carried out by companies themselves as opposed to independent organisations may have increased customer satisfaction levels but, unless the company wishes to reveal the reason for any unsatisfactory elements, real levels of dissatisfaction are not widely known. An estimation made for the purposes of this chapter suggests that there are over 20 million customer satisfaction surveys completed each year but that does not necessarily mean that companies or individuals completing them are better informed. Many consumers still need persuading that companies are reading and acting upon them.

For example, some surveys operate scales whereby those completing them can only answer using excellent, good, fair or poor categories which skews the results into the positive. Some companies like British Airways have gone to the other extreme in the past by using an eleven point scale which makes it hard for the survey responder to choose between a rating of, say, seven and eight.

Are We Complaining More?

Whether complaints are on the increase or not is the subject of some dispute. Research by Consumer Focus (*Consumer Detriment 2012*) suggested that the number of problems was declining compared to when the last survey was carried out in 2008 by the now defunct Office of Fair Trading, but this is contradicted elsewhere by data from both the private and public sectors. The Scottish Legal Complaints Commission (the Ombudsman service for complaints about the legal profession in Scotland) heard at its May 2015 monthly meeting that it had recruited extra staff to handle an increased workload. Similarly in May, the head of early resolution at the Scottish Public Services Ombudsman - which hears complaints against the Scottish Parliament, local government and public services - expressed her concern about the increased workload being placed on her staff.

One of the newer providers of complaint resolution services to businesses is a company called Ombudsman Services. It published a report in mid-August 2015 suggesting that Britons are now more likely to complain about service than Americans and it calculated that there were 66 million complaints in the last year by reference to their increasing caseload.

Whether complaints are increasing, plateauing or decreasing, it would appear that people are more ready to complain when things go wrong. These behaviours have been encouraged by a vigorous and long-established consumer movement and by both print and broadcast media exposés and readers' problem resolution sections in the consumer advocacy and testing magazine which was founded in 1957. From this and other sources people have ideas about their 'rights' and legislation such as the Sale of Goods Act and are increasingly aware of where to go to get advice and help.

Complainant Knowledge

If an item is unmerchantable many people are aware that they can complain to Trading Standards Departments in their local authorities who have considerable experience of assessing the behaviour of traders and where necessary prosecuting them when they have acted illegally.

Unsurprisingly in the light of this experience, their national body the Chartered Trading Standards Institute, (CTSI,) was appointed by the government to be responsible for assessing and certifying those alternative dispute resolution procedures that chose to apply for this (non-compulsory in the UK) stamp of approval.

If a particular business has failed to provide the remedy the consumer is looking for, the next stage is to take advice from bodies like the CAB or the local Trading Standards with a complaint which if unresolved can be escalated to an Ombudsman service if one exists for that particular market sector.

The Ombuds Business

The first Ombudsman service in the UK took its cue and the name from the Scandanavian example. It was established in 1981 by some (not all) the leading insurance companies to resolve complaints about their products and services. The financial services sector was particularly active in establishing such offices in other different market sectors such as personal investment and banking – now all brought together in the Financial Ombudsman Service (FOS) funded by companies in that sector by a levy augmented by case fees. Public sector bodies were also set up such as the Parliamentary and Health Services Ombudsman. The legal profession too has its own Ombudsman. The Financial Ombudsman has gained a particularly high profile from having to deal with widespread market failure such as the mis-selling of personal protection insurance (PPI) (an insurance which purported to assist people with for example large credit card debt in the event of their being made unemployed or suffering long-term illness). In the first six months of this year, the Financial Ombudsman Service received 162,674 new complaints on which to adjudicate of which 44,890 related to potential PPI mis-selling. (In an earlier chapter Immaculada Barral-Viñals has identified this phenomenon of large numbers of similar complaints generated in mass markets resolved in much the same sort of way as one of the situations well suited to the use of ODR).

And this will not be the last example of this form of 'mass' complaint. As the number of PPI claims diminish, a new area of mis-selling seems to be coming to the fore which will keep the name of this Ombudsman and its services firmly in the spotlight. The FOS says that packaged bank accounts which, for a fee, bundle into a bank account additional benefits such as insurance and cheaper overdrafts are a growing source of complaint. In the first six months of 2015, 25,500 people complained, more than the number which complained in the whole of 2014. So markets continue to let consumers down and increasingly consumers turn to the bodies they think will assist them – not just the established Ombudsmen but claims services which have sprung up to meet demand which an initially overwhelmed Ombudsman was seen as being unable to deal with in a timely fashion. Users of these services have to pay a proportion of the sum received in restitution to those companies. No fees are charged to the consumer by the FOS.

In the eyes of the consumer then, ombudsman services are a known resource to assist in the resolution of complaints in both the public and private sectors with which they are familiar. Consumers have now also been introduced to other providers of redress whom they may well choose to use even if they have to pay. It will pay those offering ADR schemes now and in the future to understand what drives consumers to turn their back on the free service for the more costly and more heavily promoted alternative? (Is the answer in part of the question?).

ADR - Making It Easier to Complain?

The introduction of alternative dispute resolution is believed, by those in favour of it, to have a number of benefits:

- removing some of the logjam in our courts because people will opt for this method finding it easier and cheaper than going to law

- being less intimidating than using the court system

- providing an element of independence from the companies at which the complaint is directed.

Leaving aside the problems of delay in court system, will it be less intimidating? A quasi-consumer holiday watchdog HolidayTravelWatch recently announced the results of what it called its Holiday Standards Report. Questioning a sample of 2,500 people, it found that 19% said they had been intimidated - either verbally or physically - when they had tried to make a complaint. The report found that despite 31% of Brits believing holiday standards have dropped in the last 20 years, 22% don't complain. Almost a third (30%) say they aren't confident they will get a resolution, while 27% say they don't raise the issue due to a lack of confidence. Some 19% find the process of complaining properly to be too complicated and tricky, so don't bother, while 17% say they've complained in the past and had got no or little recompense, so had given up.

Where to Go Now?

Using the long established process common to the established ombudsman systems at present can be daunting. The list of process hurdles which a complainant has to jump taken from the website of the provider Ombudsman Services is fairly typical. The service will not accept complaints where

- the customer has not first attempted to resolve the complaint directly with the trader;

- the dispute is frivolous or vexatious;

- the dispute is currently being, or has in the past been, considered by another ADR scheme or court;

- the value of the claim exceeds the maximum value of an award that can be made;

- the customer has not submitted the dispute within the required time; and

- dealing with the dispute would seriously impair the effective operation of Ombudsman Services.

Exhausting a company's processes can take a long time. Letters and e-mails can go to-and-fro. Some consumers will be sufficiently discouraged to abandon their claim.

Independence – The Key to Consumer Acceptance?

As with any resolution procedure, awareness and acceptance by the public are key to its success. One of the main drivers of acceptance in my view is independence. The law and its practitioners have a long history of independence. The introduction of ombudsmen in both the public and private sectors was also seen as providing an independent arbitrator when the people had complaints. But some services set up to address the concerns of the public even when positioned as being independent have not been viewed as such. The obvious recent UK case is that of the former self-regulatory Press Complaints Commission (PCC) now seen as being dominated in the past by the press magnates who passed judgement upon themselves, their editors and their staff favouring their own interests and not those of their readers. After the general loss of public confidence following the Leveson enquiry and court cases associated with the hacking of mobile phones by certain journalists or sub-contractors the Independent Press Standards Organisation (IPSO) was set up to restore public confidence, designed to function in a way that addressed the lack of independence of the previous body.

Tear It Down and Start Again

Sometimes an organisation is performing an independent role and its annual report and statistics may confirm that many cases have been decided. But I contend that if the public has a perception that it is not independent or is even biased towards the industry that it regulates then a significant change is required to alter that perception. The decision by publishers to close the PCC and set up IPSO may have calmed those doubts in this sector of the market but it shows the lengths that discredited organisations must go in order to restore confidence – tear it down and start again.

Too Close for Comfort?

There is a risk that similar perception issues may materialise if the new ADR organisations are not considered independent of the organisations whose activities they scrutinise. The Civil Aviation Authority (CAA) has operated a complaints procedure for some years on behalf of passengers against airlines. They also operate the bonding system – ATOL – which offers redress if an ATOL bonded tour operator (a packager of all the elements of a holiday – flight, hotel) goes into liquidation. Originally it was believed that the CAA planned to set up its own dispute resolution system but it decided that it would not be perceived as being independent so it is seeking an independent provider through a public tender.

This is in contrast to the process favoured by ABTA, the travel trade association that numbers tour operators and travel agents amongst its members. The association announced in July 2015, that its ADR service had been duly certified by CTSI in advance of the October 1st deadline and that they were able to proclaim that their scheme as the 'first and only' ADR scheme designed specifically for member travel companies and their clients. Complainants must first complain to the company, then to ABTA and, if ABTA cannot resolve the issue, then the complainant is referred to a company appointed by it to provide an ADR Arbitration service. This is in essence the process used by ABTA since the early days of Office of Fair Trading-sponsored codes of practice whereby the trade association took responsibility for escalated complaint handling concerning problems faced by their members, now adapted to comply with the new ADR arrangements and given the OK by the authority competent to do so. The question is whether consumers will go the full distance with the ABTA scheme designed specifically for member travel companies (and only for them) with a long experience of that market sector - prioritising that historic capability over any concerns about abstract values such as independence. This underlines how important it will be for consumers to be well-informed about the rigour and scope of ADR scheme registration and the integrity of the process of registration and subsequent monitoring. Equally business and their trade bodies will have to understand their responsibilities to inform complainants about the appropriate certified, registered schemes. (For a full account of these arrangements and the responsibilities they impose, see the chapter by Pablo Cortés).

Competition and choice can offer risky options for the complainant. Evidence from the travel market in Germany shows increasing competition between the established industry arbitration scheme 'söp' (Schlictungstelle für den öffentlichen Personenverkehr e.V.). Here the claims companies are aggressively marketing their services by recommending the court route as being more likely to yield higher damages even if that sum is reduced by their fees. Less time, more money are tempting marketing propositions.

How Will the Public Judge Who Is Best?

Most of the established ombudsman-type organisations have been resolving complaints for some time. The FOS staff are specialised in both in terms of the products and services of the markets where the consumer problems originate. How easy is it for those working in a service operating across a diverse market sectors to manage complaints to a conclusion? One such company says that it is specialised in five areas as disparate as copyright, energy and property and can assist in another four. Will these multi-sector concerns satisfy their customers of their competence across all of those sectors? Will the fact that a single provider of dispute resolution service sour consumers' expectations of fairness and independence? Only time will tell if consumers will begin pressing traders to offer a choice of dispute resolution options.

One other element will be important for the future – financial stability. It is not an accident that the UK's most established ombudsman/ADR schemes are in markets where many of the players have deep pockets – financial services are the obvious example. These are expensive schemes to run. They also enjoy the advantages of being the only game in town with 100% sign up from practitioners – it helps to have statutory backing. Less well favoured Ombudsman schemes such as the Funeral Ombudsman have foundered in the past. How will the new competition fare in less settled market conditions?

Competition – Who and How?

One development in the market is of particular interest here. As we have seen with the PPI example as the number of disputes exploded, claims agencies arose to work for consumer redress by taking a fee if the outcome was successful – a conditional fee arrangement offered by conventional legal practitioners as well. Some law firms have entered this market using the new business model of Alternative Business Structures allowing them to partner with other businesses (even supermarkets) to set up agencies, often at arms' length, in order to retain or gain some of the business that might otherwise have gone to the other ADR providers. Do legal practitioners and therefore businesses with a declared link to them enjoy a reputational advantage over other providers that will translate into competitive advantage? Will the marketing claims encourage unrealistic expectations amongst complainants?

Resolution timescales

Will the measure of 'time to close complaints' also be significant? Escalated complaints can drag on for a very long time. The time spent exhausting a company's procedures can be considerable and the decision from the Ombudsman is not exactly speedy. The latest figures from the Legal Ombudsman for England and Wales shows that only about a third of cases are resolved within 56 days and about two-thirds in 90 days: the FOS manages 94% in 8 weeks. Consumer confidence will be increased if the alternative disputes resolution system functions faster than going to law or any of the other options available. The new regulations give 90 days as the time limit.

Many US-based dispute resolution specialists resolve cases in hours rather than days or weeks. The public will certainly be looking for early resolution. Companies who can demonstrate past achievement of complaint resolution within this shorter timeframe may be at an advantage in the eyes of the consumer. However the reality is that 'the time to close' metric reflects the complexity and value of the case – the higher the stakes the more complex and lengthy the process. Case closure is not just a measure of the efficiency of the process of resolution as demonstrated in Amy Koltz's chapter looking at the management of complex cases involving home repossession. The stakes could not be higher and while the introduction of elements of online dispute resolution can help improve the quality of case management with better inter-party communication and aspects of document organisation, that is not the principal determinant of the time taken. However if online dispute resolution on a more or less automated basis is to be available for the low value or what the Laboratory of Cyberjustice at the University of Montreal calls low intensity disputes (as referenced by Riika Koulu's chapter) then consumers can legitimately expect swifter closure.

Public Perception Rules

I have made the point that the success of an alternative dispute resolution system depends on how the public perceives it. If the public considers that those offering a resolution service are too close to the companies or organisation to which the complaint is directed, then they will question its independence and avoid the process in which case the government's desire to provide an alternative to the courts system will be at risk. Another important source for evidence of competence in the public's mind may be the percentage of cases decided in the consumer's favour. The FOS currently resolves an average of just 57% in favour of the consumer– it also publishes company by company outcomes showing that % of cases involving Bank X are resolved this way or another. Should the consumer choose the ADR service that 'wins' ie finds for the consumer most often? Consumers need to understand that repeated findings in the complainant's favour in respect of a particular company or market sector may be less of an indication of the ADR provider's heart being in the right place than the poor quality of service being provided by the company in the first place. ADR systems are not in and of themselves consumer champions, exponents of the 'For the Consumer Right or Wrong' philosophy – they have been set up to give the consumer better access to resolution but not to guarantee that the outcome will always favour them. ADR schemes have a difficult balance to sustain between rigour in regard to the evidence and responsiveness to those in need of resolution of their problems.

Much will depend on the satisfactory bedding down of the system of registration whether carried out by ITSA or one of the other seven Competent Authorities. Will certification be a reliable guide to quality for the user of ADR schemes? Will these schemes meet those criteria of:

- Access

- Expertise, independence and impartiality

- Transparency

- Effectiveness

- Fairness

- Legality?

Take Away Points

1. The UK complaint handling market is quite mature with some dominant established players with statutory backing in certain

markets. New entrants may face stiff competition but there are precedents for claims agencies taking some of the established players' business.

2. There have been examples of the sort of 'mass complaint' that would favour the introduction of automated systems of online dispute resolution

3. It is hard to anticipate how complainants will take to the new ADR arrangements and what elements of the offer they will be swayed by. Will it be abstract notions of independence or the marketing promises of decisions in less time, with more money from decisions more often in their favour? How realistic is that?

4. Much depends on the quality of the registration scheme and how good a guide certification will be to the ADR schemes certified by the Competent Authorities

About the Authors

Marc Grainer

 Marc Grainer received a BA from University of Michigan in 1969 and a JD from Harvard Law School in 1972.

Since the 1970's, he has managed hundred's of customer care projects in a wide range of industries throughout the world. The aim of this work has always been to identify those strategies that return the highest ROI's.

Mr. Grainer was the principal author of the White House and Customer Rage studies that are the basis for this chapter. He is presently Chairman of Customer Care Measurement and Consulting, an Alexandria, VA firm, offering services in all aspects of the customer experience.

Mr. Grainer also acknowledges the contributions to the chapter of Scott Brotzmann, David Beinhacker, and Richard Grainer.

Jo DeMars

Jo DeMars is president and owner of DeMars & Associates. She develops the vision for her company by utilizing her unique background in consumer education, regulation, and public policy development combined with years of management expertise. An accomplished mediator and arbitrator, she has designed and conducted training programs on the principles of arbitration for more than twenty-five years.

DeMars has been a frequent speaker at national and international conferences. In 1995, DeMars received the Entrepreneurial Woman of the Year Award from Wisconsin Women Entrepreneurs and was recognized in 2005 as a Woman of Distinction by the Waukesha County Foundation.

Pablo Cortés

Dr Pablo Cortés is a Senior Lecturer at University of Leicester's School of Law. He is currently on research leave (2014/16) while completing two projects: a European grant to research on online mediation and a Nuffield grant to evaluate consumer ADR schemes in the EU. He has been invited to expert meetings and advised the UNCITRAL (WG3), the European Commission (DG SANCO) and (DG JUST), the European Parliament (IMCO) and (JURI). He is a fellow of the NCTDR (UMass) and in 2012 he was a Gould Research Fellow at Stanford University.

Immaculada Barral-Viñals

Immaculada Barral-Viñals is a Law PH.D, and Professor of Private law, University of Barcelona, since 1997. Presently is Salvador Madariaga fellow at the Ciberjustice laboratory, Centre de Recherche en Droit Public, University of Montréal. She is Director of Advanced Research (AQU)-2007; and Member of Institut de Dret i Tecnologia –Law and technology institute- of the Autonomous University of Barcelona (IDT-UAB).

From 2002 on she is arbitror at the Arbitral Chamber of the Catalan Agency for Consumers. In 2009-2011 she was the Director of the Working Group on consumer mediation, White Book of Mediation in Catalonia (www.llibreblancmediacio.com). Presently she is a member of the IMI task force on ODR, and of the Catalan Legislative Committee for legislation (Comissió de Codificació de Catalunya).

Riika Koulu

Riikka Koulu (LL.M. trained on the bench) is a doctoral candidate of procedural law at the University of Helsinki. In her theoretically oriented doctoral dissertation Dispute Resolution and Technology: Revisiting Justification, she focuses on the implications of implementing technology into dispute resolution and enforcement, illustrating how this shift creates the need for new legal interpretations and concepts. In addition, her research interests include Internet governance, Science and Technology Studies and critical systems theory. Her earlier publications concern e.g. cross-border civil procedure (2015), justification of ODR (2014), doctrines of dispute resolution and technology (2013), access to Internet (2012) and video-conferencing (2010, 2011).

Amy Koltz

Amy H. Koltz, J.D. is Executive Director and Mediator for Metro Milwaukee Mediation Services, Inc. Ms. Koltz is an Adjunct Professor at Marquette University Law School. She mediates for the U.S. Bankruptcy Courts of the Eastern & Western Districts of Wisconsin. She is a Past-Chairperson and current member of the Wisconsin State Bar's Dispute Resolution Section Board. Ms. Koltz formerly served as Process & Compliance Manager for DeMars & Associates, Ltd.

Ms. Koltz earned a B.A. from The College of William and Mary, a J.D. from Marquette University Law School, and a Graduate Certificate in Dispute Resolution from Marquette University School of Professional Studies.

Katherine G. Newcomer

Katherine Newcomer is a member of the New Jersey Bar. Currently, her practice deals with high conflict mediation, and arbitration. Her experience in Dispute Resolution and Arbitration is extensive. She has decided over two hundred cases for Net Neutrals. She has conducted hearings and written decisions for Arbitration programs for DeMars and Associates, Ltd.

She graduated cum laude from Drew University, Madison, New Jersey with a B.A. She spent her senior year abroad at Ripon Hall, Oxford University, United Kingdom. She graduated from Rutgers – The State University, School of Law, Newark, with a J.D.

She served on numerous non-profit boards and is very active in a state-wide mediation association. She has recently published an historical fiction novel entitled "The Phoenix and the Falcon."

Adrian Lawes

Educated in Wales and Australia, Adrian worked in market research and publishing in both Australia and the UK before part-founding a company, Consumerdata Ltd, 22 years ago, that specialises in travel customer satisfaction measurement. It is recognised as a market leader in the UK and Europe and its reach extends across the globe with our technology in over 30 countries. For the last five years Adrian has also edited *Just about Travel*.

Colin Adamson

Born in India and educated in Scotland, Colin Adamson is a leading European specialist consultant in customer service, complaint handling and consumer affairs. He has advised government, public sector organisations as well as major companies and professional bodies in the UK and abroad, undertaking projects to improve customer service and complaint handling with companies in the EC, Eastern Europe, Australia and the Far East in the areas of customer response and service quality. In the UK he organised a series of research studies for a number of Ombudsman offices. He is a founder member and past Chair of the Society of Consumer Affairs Professionals (SOCAP) and set up the European offices of TARP the US specialist complaint management and customer satisfaction measurement consultancy.

Printed in the United States
By Bookmasters